International Labour and Employment Compliance Handbook

www.kluwerlawonline.com

Labour and Employment Compliance in Israel

International Bar Association

Labour and Employment Compliance in Israel

Fifth Edition

Yaron Horovitz
Pnina Broder-Manor
Helen Raziel

This publication is part of the International Labour and Employment Compliance Handbook, available on www.kluwerlawonline.com

Editors: Salvador del Rey and Robert J. Mignin

the global voice of the legal profession

Wolters Kluwer

Published by:
Kluwer Law International B.V.
PO Box 316
2400 AH Alphen aan den Rijn
The Netherlands
E-mail: international-sales@wolterskluwer.com
Website: lrus.wolterskluwer.com

Sold and distributed in North, Central and South America by:
Wolters Kluwer Legal & Regulatory U.S.
7201 McKinney Circle
Frederick, MD 21704
United States of America
Email: customer.service@wolterskluwer.com

Sold and distributed in all other countries by:
Air Business Subscriptions
Rockwood House
Haywards Heath
West Sussex
RH16 3DH
United Kingdom
Email: international-customerservice@wolterskluwer.com

ISBN 978-94-035-0430-8

e-Book: ISBN 978-94-035-0431-5
web-PDF: ISBN 978-94-035-0432-2

All listed titles are also available on lrus.wolterskluwer.com

1. Argentina: Julio César Stefanoni Zani & Enrique Alfredo Betemps, *Labour and Employment Compliance in Argentina, 6th edition*, 2018 (ISBN 978-94-035-0373-8)
2. Australia: John Tuck, Stephen Price, Rosemary Roach, Jack de Flamingh, Nicholas Ellery & Nick Le Mare, *Labour and Employment Compliance in Australia, 3rd edition*, 2018 (ISBN 978-94-035-0380-6)
3. Belgium: Chris Van Olmen, *Labour and Employment Compliance in Belgium, 3rd edition*, 2018 (ISBN 978-94-035-0383-7)
4. Brazil: Rodrigo Seizo Takano, Andrea Giamondo Massei Rossi & Murilo Caldeira Germiniani, *Labour and Employment Compliance in Brazil, 5th edition*, 2018 (ISBN 978-94-035-0390-5)
5. Canada: Kevin Coon & Adrian Ishak, *Labour and Employment Compliance in Canada, 2nd edition*, 2014 (ISBN 978-90-411-5637-2)
6. Chile: Gerardo Otero A., Maria Dolores Echeverria F., Macarena López M. & María de los Ángeles Fernández S., *Labour and Employment Compliance in Chile, 6th edition*, 2018 (ISBN 978-94-035-0393-6)
7. China: King & Wood Mallesons, *Labour and Employment Compliance in China, 5th edition*, 2018 (ISBN 978-94-035-0400-1)
8. England: Tony Hyams-Parish, *Labour and Employment Compliance in England, 6th edition*, 2018 (ISBN 978-94-035-0403-2)
9. France: Pascale Lagesse, *Labour and Employment Compliance in France, 6th edition*, 2018 (ISBN 978-94-035-0410-0)
10. Germany: Gerlind Wisskirchen & Martin Lützeler, *Labour and Employment Compliance in Germany, 6th edition*, 2018 (ISBN 978-94-035-0413-1)
11. India: Manishi Pathak, *Labour and Employment Compliance in India, 6th edition*, 2018 (ISBN 978-94-035-0420-9)
12. Ireland: Duncan Inverarity & Sinéad Grace, *Labour and Employment Compliance in Ireland, 5th edition*, 2018 (ISBN 978-94-035-0423-0)
13. Israel: Yaron Horovitz, Pnina Broder-Manor & Helen Raziel, *Labour and Employment Compliance in Israel, 5th edition*, 2018 (ISBN 978-94-035-0430-8)
14. Italy: Angelo Zambelli, *Labour and Employment Compliance in Italy, 6th edition*, 2018 (ISBN 978-94-035-0433-9)
15. Japan: Yoshikazu Sugino, *Labour and Employment Compliance in Japan, 6th edition*, 2018 (ISBN 978-94-035-0440-7)
16. Republic of Korea: Sang Wook Cho, Soojung Lee & Christopher Mandel, *Labour and Employment Compliance in the Republic of Korea, 4th edition*, 2018 (ISBN 978-94-035-0453-7)
17. Mexico: Oscar De La Vega Gómez, *Labour and Employment Compliance in Mexico, 6th edition*, 2018 (ISBN 978-94-035-0443-8)
18. The Netherlands: Els de Wind & Cara Pronk, *Labour and Employment Compliance in the Netherlands, 4th edition*, 2018 (ISBN 978-94-035-0470-4)
19. Poland: Barbara Jóźwik, *Labour and Employment Compliance in Poland, 6th edition*, 2018 (ISBN 978-94-035-0450-6)

20. Russia: Anna-Stefaniya Chepik, *Labour and Employment Compliance in Russia*, 2013 (ISBN 978-90-411-4925-1)
21. Saudi Arabia: Sara Khoja & Sarit Thomas, *Labour and Employment Compliance in Saudi Arabia, 1st edition,* 2018 (ISBN 978-94-035-0490-2)
22. South Africa: Susan Stelzner, Stuart Harrison, Brian Patterson & Zahida Ebrahim, *Labour and Employment Compliance in South Africa, 6th edition*, 2018 (ISBN 978-94-035-0460-5)
23. Spain: Salvador del Rey & Ana Campos, *Labour and Employment Compliance in Spain, 6th edition*, 2018 (978-94-035-0463-6)
24. Turkey: Sertaç Kökenek & Elif Nur Çakır, *Labour and Employment Compliance in Turkey, 4th edition*, 2018 (ISBN 978-94-035-0473-5)
25. United Arab Emirates: Sara Khoja & Sarit Thomas, *Labour and Employment Compliance in the United Arab Emirates, 5th edition*, 2018 (ISBN 978-94-035-0480-3)
26. United States: Baker & McKenzie LLP, *Labour and Employment Compliance in the United States, 4th edition*, 2018 (ISBN 978-94-035-0483-4)

International Bar Association
The Global Voice of the Legal Profession

The International Bar Association (IBA), established in 1947, is the world's leading organization of international legal practitioners, bar associations and law societies. The IBA influences the development of international law reform and shapes the future of the legal profession throughout the world. It has a membership of over 40,000 individual lawyers and almost 200 bar associations and law societies spanning all continents. It has considerable expertise in providing assistance to the global legal community.

Grouped into two divisions – the Legal Practice Division and the Public and Professional Interest Division – the IBA covers all practice areas and professional interests, providing members with access to leading experts and up-to-date information. Through the various committees of the divisions, the IBA enables an interchange of information and views among its members as to laws, practices and professional responsibilities relating to the practice of business law around the globe. Additionally, the IBA's high-quality publications and world-class conferences provide unrivalled professional development and network-building opportunities for international legal practitioners and professional associates.

The IBA's Bar Issues Commission provides an invaluable forum for IBA member organisations to discuss all matters relating to law at an international level.

The IBA's Human Rights Institute (IBAHRI) works across the Association, to promote, protect and enforce human rights under a just rule of law, and to preserve the independence of the judiciary and the legal profession worldwide.

Other institutions established by the IBA include the Southern Africa Litigation Centre and the International Legal Assistance Consortium.

Employment and Industrial Relations Law Committee

The aims of the committee are to develop and exchange knowledge of employment and industrial relations law and practice. Members support each other through the provision of innovative ideas and practical assistance on day-to-day issues. In addition, through its journal and through presentations, conferences, the committee ensures the dissemination of up-to-date law and practice in this highly important business area.

International Bar Association Global Employment Institute

The IBA Global Employment Institute (IBA GEI) was formed in early 2010 for the purpose of developing for multinationals and worldwide institutions a global and strategic approach to the key legal issues in the human resources and human capital fields.

Drawing on the resources and expertise of the IBA membership, the IBA GEI will provide a unique contribution in the field of employment, discrimination and immigration law, on a diverse range of global issues, to private and public organizations throughout the world. The IBA GEI is designed to enhance the management, performance and productivity of these organizations and help achieve best practice in their human capital and management functions from a strategic perspective.

The IBA GEI will become the leading voice and authority on global HR issues by virtue of having a number of the world's leading labour and employment practitioners in its ranks, and the support and resource of the world's largest association of international lawyers.

Further information

International Bar Association, 4th Floor, 10 St Bride Street, London EC4A 4AD, United Kingdom, Tel: +44 (0)20 7842 0090, Fax: +44 (0)20 7842 0091, E-mail: member@int-bar.org, www.ibanet.org

About the International Labour and Employment Compliance Handbook

From 1976 through 1988, the International Bar Association and Kluwer Law International published the groundbreaking International Handbook on Contracts of Employment. This Handbook provided one of the first global overviews of the law of the international employment relationship.

Since publishing the first edition, globalization of business has created an increased demand for knowledge of labor and employment laws throughout the world. Therefore, along with Kluwer, we decided to publish an updated Handbook which we have titled the International Labour and Employment Compliance Handbook.

This new Handbook was intended to be a practical guide by providing a general overview of key labor and employment issues in multiple jurisdictions. Each chapter was written so that it is easy to understand by lawyers and non-lawyers alike. Each country author has also followed a standard outline to assist readers in analysing employment issues in each country.

The first edition of this new Handbook included nineteen (19) different countries.

This Handbook would not have been possible without the help and assistance of many people. Most importantly, the individual country authors are all distinguished legal practitioners who spent considerable time drafting and revising their country reports to meet difficult deadlines. We thank each of them. Our friends at Kluwer, especially Ewa Szkatula, have done a wonderful job in keeping the editors and the authors on schedule. Finally, we want to also express our gratitude to Cuatrecasas, Gonçalves Pereira, and Baker & McKenzie LLP for their valuable assistance in the coordination and organization of this project. Our warmest thanks to each of them.

Because of the success of the Handbook,Wolters Kluwer Law & Business decided to publish each country report also as a separate book to give a choice in obtaining the information. We hope this new format will be a helpful and useful resource just like the Handbook. Both formats are available in print and online.

The Editors

Salvador del Rey Guanter
Robert J. Mignin

March 2013

Israel

AUTHORS

Yaron Horovitz, Adv.

As from 1 January 2017, Mr Horovitz resigned as a partner with the firm to establish within the firm a new practice as a mediator for dispute resolutions of all kinds – domestic and international – while seeking to focus on labor and employment law, corporate and commercial law. While no longer a member of the firm, Mr Horovitz continues to work from the firm's Tel-Aviv office.

Prior to his resignation, Mr Horovitz was a partner located in the Tel-Aviv office from 1 January 1997 having joined the firm in 1990. Prior to joining the firm, Mr Horovitz clerked for the Israel Supreme Court and with another leading law firm in Israel.

While at the firm Mr Horovitz represented local and multinational private and public companies, many of them in the high-tech industry, governmental entities and select employee groups (such as airline pilots and physicians' organizations) – and headed up the labour and employment law fields in Naschitz Brandes.

Born in Jerusalem, Mr Horovitz received his LL.B. (cum laude) from the Hebrew University in Jerusalem, Israel in 1989 and his LL.M. from the London School of Economics and Political Science in 1995, and was admitted to practice law in Israel in 1990. Mr Horovitz is fluent in English and Hebrew.

ADDRESS

Naschitz, Brandes, Amir & Co.,
Advocates, 5, Tuval Street,
Tel-Aviv 67897,
Israel

Tel.: +972-3-623-5000;
+972-3-623-5070
Fax: +972-3-623-5081
E-mail: yhorovitz@nblaw.com
Web: <www.nblaw.com>

Pnina Broder-Manor

Ms Broder-Manor is a partner located in the Tel-Aviv office. She joined the firm in 1992 and has been a partner since 1 January 2001. Ms Broder-Manor clerked for the Israel Supreme Court.

Ms Broder-Manor represents commercial clients, both private companies in various stages of development and public companies. She represents clients situated in Israel and abroad, including multinational companies. Ms Broder-Manor provides a range of services and has experience in the fields of labour and employment law, corporate law, contracts, finance, international transactions, real estate and dispute resolution.

She has over twenty years of practical experience in all aspects of employment law and has advised employers over a wide range of issues. Ms Broder-Manor has advised local and international clients and often issues advice to non-Israeli law firms on various aspects of Israeli labour laws. She has extensive experience in advising on the employment aspects of mergers and acquisitions.

Ms Broder-Manor also has substantial experience in matters of employment law and immigration. She has advised several international clients in relation to the employment of foreign individuals – advising them on the processes involved and assisting them in approaching the relevant government authorities in Israel in obtaining such permits as may be required in any given instance. She has particular expertise in assisting with foreign expert entry and work permits for employees of international clients.

Ms Broder-Manor is the partner representing Naschitz Brandes Amir as the Israeli member of the Employment Law Alliance (ELA). Her involvement in the ELA and attendance at its various meetings and conferences assists in keeping up with trends and issues at the international level.

Born in Montreal, Ms Broder-Manor received her LL.B. degree from Tel-Aviv University in 1989 and was admitted to practice law in Israel in 1990. She is fluent in English and Hebrew.

ADDRESS

Naschitz, Brandes, Amir & Co.,
Advocates, 5, Tuval Street,
Tel-Aviv 67897,

Israel
Tel.: +972-3-623-5160
Fax: +972-3-623-5170
E-mail: pbroder@nblaw.com
Web: <www.nblaw.com>

Helen Raziel

Ms Raziel is a partner located in the Tel-Aviv office. Her practice embraces a broad range of fields –corporate and commercial law, hi-tech and bio-tech financing (private financings), intellectual property, public utilities law (water and electricity) and public tenders. Ms. Raziel advises on litigation issues for overseas clients in numerous commercial contexts and has been involved in international arbitration work (ICC and other).

Ms Raziel has been with the firm since 2000. Prior to that, after arriving in Israel, she completed her internship and then worked as an attorney with another major commercial law firm in Tel-Aviv, where she handled a broad range of commercial issues.

Ms Raziel acts for a wide range of local and international clients and advises on all aspects of their business in Israel. Ms Raziel has considerable experience in advising on the entire range of employment law and often is required to respond quickly to day-to-day employment law queries raised by clients during the course of their business as well as dealing with employment law issues, which arise in the merger and acquisition context. Ms Raziel also provides regular legal advice on Israeli employment laws to foreign law firms.

Before coming to Israel, Ms Raziel was both a qualified barrister at the Bar of England and Wales and a lecturer in law at the University of Buckingham, England. During her time at the Bar, Ms Raziel was one of the legal team appointed to assist a major public inquiry in London, England into the failings of the social services in one of the major child abuse cases of the 1980s.

Ms Raziel is a member of the Israel British Lawyers Association.

Born in Bristol, England, Ms Raziel received her LL.B. (cum laude) from the University of East Anglia, England in 1981 and her LL.M. from the London School of Economics and Political Science in 1982. Ms Raziel was called to the Bar of England and Wales in 1984, and was admitted to practice law in Israel in 1990. Her mother tongue is English but she also speaks Hebrew.

ADDRESS

Naschitz, Brandes, Amir & Co.,
Advocates, 5, Tuval Street,

Tel-Aviv 67897,
Israel

Tel.: +972-3-623-5000
+972-3-623-5065,
Fax: +972-3-623-5051
E-mail: hraziel@nblaw.com
Web: <www.nblaw.com>

Naschitz Brandes, Amir & Co
Firm Overview

Naschitz, Brandes, Amir & Co is one of the leading and most prestigious full-service law firms in Israel with an international and domestic practice that embraces virtually the entire spectrum of civil matters. The firm is well known for its expertise and experience in the field of employment and labour law.

It comprises over 150 legal professionals consistently recognized as leaders in their respective fields. The firm strives to provide sophisticated, innovated and practical advice and prides itself on combining expert knowledge of the law, familiarity with market practice, zealous dedication to its clients' interests and the highest standards of professional ethics.

All of Naschitz Brandes' partners and many of its lawyers are multilingual and many have qualified and practised as lawyers in USA, and England.

Scope of this Guide

This Guide is of general, overview nature only and aims to highlight items solely for information purposes. This Guide does not purport to offer legal advice nor should be deemed as offering legal advice and/or as a substitute to taking full and proper legal advice on any of the matters dealt with herein.

This Guide was originally prepared during the last part of 2010 and early 2011 and has since been updated so as to provide only a general overview, with the most recent update as at May 2018.

For further information on any of the fields covered by this Guide, you are invited to contact the following individuals at Naschitz, Brandes, Amir:

Ms Pnina Broder-Manor, Adv., E-mail: pbroder@nblaw.com; Ms Helen Raziel, Adv., E-mail: hraziel@nblaw.com.

Naschitz, Brandes, Amir accepts no liability with respect to the accuracy or otherwise of any information contained in this Guide.

Legal Compliance in Israel

Legal Compliance in Israel

1. LEGAL FRAMEWORK: EMPLOYMENT LAWS IN ISRAEL

Israeli employment law is drawn from a number of legal sources:

- legislation – both primary and secondary and including not only strictly labour law directed but also more general legislation;
- collective agreements – collective arrangements and extension orders thereof;
- individual employment agreements/custom and practice.

Where there is a contradiction between different sources, the general approach adopted by the Labour Courts is to take that which is more favourable to the employee. The legal sources are interpreted by the Labour Court, the main judicial body developing labour law (and in some cases creating new norms and mandatory practices). It should also be noted that international standards (the ILO conventions adopted by Israel and also EU standards) are used as guidelines by the Labour Courts even though they are not binding.

During the earlier years of its establishment, Israel was a country with socialist orientation. The General Federation of Workers in Israel (the 'Histadrut') played an influential and important role in the early development of labour laws in Israel. In addition to providing direct membership to blue and white collar unions, the Histadrut provided social services – health care, pensions, insurance schemes, sports and cultural activities, etc. The Histadrut was an integral part of the labour movement, which formed the government coalitions until 1977. The influence of the Histadrut combined with the ideology of the labour movement led to the adoption of a comprehensive system of employee protective legislation for employment laws. The union density was high and remained so until the 1990s.

This high union density resulted in collective agreements governing most large workplaces. The preference was to keep the courts out of the area of collective labour law – resulting in a model of State non-intervention in this area. The legislation governing collective labour law is the Collective Agreements Law, 1957 and the Settlement of Labour Disputes Law, 1957. Until the early 1970s, there were no limits on strikes and the law gave unions and strikers protection for strike activity.

In the early 1970s (with the adoption of the Labour Courts' Law, 1969), the Labour Courts were established. The Labour Courts have made a significant contribution to the development of labour law in Israel. For example, the Labour Courts have contributed to the stabilization of labour relations and settlement of collective disputes through negotiation and adjudication. They also interpret collective and individual agreements and reside over cases involving employee rights.

During the 1990s, the socialist basis of the society changed – the high union density declined. As from 1 January 1995, the Compulsory National Health Insurance Law entered into force, which guaranteed medical coverage to every resident. This in itself brought about a substantial overnight reduction in Histadrut membership. While the Histadrut still holds a prominent position, there are also other important employee unions – the Teachers' Unions (Grade School and High School), the Doctors' Union and the Leumit National General Union.

The main employment law legislation (not in any particular order) includes the following legislation by way of example:

- Notification to an Employee and Job Candidate (Terms of Employment and Screening and Recruitment Process) Law, 2002.
- Advance Notice for Dismissal and Resignation Law, 2001.
- Hours of Works and Rest Law, 1951.
- Minimum Wage Law, 1957.
- Wages Protection Law, 1958.
- Annual Vacation Law, 1951.
- Sick Pay Law, 1976.
- Employment of Women Law, 1954.
- Employment Equal Opportunities Law, 1988.
- Equal Wages Law, 1996.
- Severance Pay Law, 1963.
- Enhancement of Enforcement Law, 2011.

Much of the employment law legislation sets forth fundamental and minimum employee entitlements. These laws apply to all employees (subject only to specific exceptions).

In addition to the legislation, a large part of the employees' rights as well as their obligations are included within the framework of collective agreements. By virtue of the Collective Agreements Law, 1957, these agreements have acquired a special status and the employee unions and employers have been granted wide legal powers to determine legal norms. Accordingly, collective agreements constitute a source of employment law. In the event of a contradiction between the provisions of a collective agreement and those of an individual employment agreement, the former will take precedence, unless the employment agreement improves upon the rights of the employee provided under the collective agreement.

The Collective Agreements Law 1957 also empowers the Minister of Economy and Industry to extend collective agreements using extension orders. By means of these extension orders, collective agreements can apply to employers and employees who are not members of those particular unions which are parties to the collective agreements themselves. Extension orders have normative effect and have been frequently issued. The extension orders may apply to the general work force (such as the extension order regarding pension rights – see further at sections 5.2 and 11.2 below) or may be directed only to a specific sector within the work force. While it is still true to say that, in the main, the Israeli hi-tech industry operates such that much of the terms of employment are set forth in the individual employment agreements, subject of course to the mandatory provisions of Israeli employment law, there has been increased employee union involvement in that industry in more recent years.

As a general rule, the employee rights and entitlements given by mandatory provisions of law, extension orders and collective agreements (whether general or specific) are overriding and the parties to the individual employment relationship cannot waive them or derogate from them. However, the parties are free to improve upon the minimum entitlements.

The decisions of the Labour Courts are also a source of law in the interpretation of the various legislative measures and also the terms of individual employment agreements. In addition, the Labour Courts may go so far as to create new norms or mandatory procedures (such as, for example, the right of the employee in the private sector to a hearing before a decision to terminate the employment has been reached by the employer – see further sections 5 and 6 below). It is worth noting that the general approach of the Israeli Labour Courts is that it is more likely that an order to reinstate an employee would be made in the public sector whereas this is less likely in the case of employment relationships within the private sector (although more recent case law has found it appropriate to make such an order in certain cases).

Apart from the specific legislation addressing employment law issues, other more general laws may also be relevant in considering employment law issues. For example, Contracts (General Part) Law – 1973, Contracts (Remedies for Breach of Contract) Law – 1970, Restrictive Trade Practices

Law – 1988, Civil Wrongs Ordinance [New Version] – 1968, Commercial Torts Law – 1999, Basic Law: Human Dignity and Liberty.

One important element to bear in mind, when considering employment relations under Israeli law, is the general duty of the parties to the contract to act in good faith and in the customary manner (as required under sections 12 and 39 of the Contracts (General Part) Law 1973). This duty – which is a 'golden thread' running throughout Israeli contracts law – applies to the negotiation, performance and termination of contracts of all kinds (including employment contracts). With respect to contractual negotiations, the duty of good faith requires that each party disclose to the other party relevant information and even information that the other party could have determined on its own. In the employment context, the duty on the parties is higher than that imposed in a regular commercial context.

Another, more general, aspect of Israeli law, which should be mentioned, is the interpretation of contacts under Israeli law. Section 25 of the Contracts (General Part) Law 1973, which was amended in 2011, reads, in amended part, as follows:

> *Section 25 (1) (a) A contract will be interpreted according to the intentions of the parties, as it appears from the contract and the circumstances of the matter, and where the intentions of the parties appears expressly from the language of the contract, the contract will be interpreted according to its language. ...*
> *Section (B1) Where a contract is capable of different interpretations and one of the parties had preference in the drafting of its terms, the interpretation against such party will be preferred interpretation in such party's favour.*

These statutory rules of interpretation of contracts, will also apply to the employment context.

2. CONTRACTS OF EMPLOYMENT

2.1. Overview

Under Israeli law, the general rule is that there is no legislative requirement for an employment contract to be in writing. Indeed, there are many instances of employment where no formal written agreement is used. Moreover, there is no single labour law regulating individual labour contracts rather, different laws provide minimum employee protective requirements. Accordingly, the general Israeli laws as to contracts (the Contracts (General Parts) Law 1973 and the Contracts (Remedies for Breach of Contract) Law 1970) apply to employment contracts just as they do to other contracts (including, as noted above, the duty to act in good faith and in the customary manner). It should be noted that the general remedies under Israeli contracts law would not operate to derogate from any specific mandatory minimum entitlements provided under employment laws (e.g., the requirement to pay severance pay upon termination where the same is required by law).

Notwithstanding the above, pursuant to the Notification to an Employee and Job Candidate (Terms of Employment and Screening and Recruitment Process) Law 2002, employers are obliged to provide their employees with detailed written notification of certain terms of employment (these are spelt out in section 2.2 below). The law further imposes an obligation to provide the employee with written notification of certain changes to the terms of employment and was further amended during 2014 to also include an obligation on employers to send notifications to employee candidates as to progress in the employment application process (see section 3.8 below).

Israeli law distinguishes between employment for an indefinite term and employment for a defined or fixed term. In case of employment for a fixed term, the employment expires at the end of the fixed term, without notice. Where the employer terminates a fixed-term employment agreement before the expiration of the term, without cause, the termination will be considered a breach of contract and the employer may be liable for compensation up to the remuneration the employee would have received had the employment not been terminated. It should be noted that, upon the expiration of the fixed term, severance pay will still be due and payable, in accordance with the provisions of the Severance Pay Law (as to which see further below at Section 5.2 below). With reference to cases of termination of an employment for an indefinite term, see further at sections 5 and 6 below.

Where a collective agreement applies to the employment relationship in question, the terms and conditions of that collective agreement will need to be taken into account in determining the respective rights and obligations of the parties, in addition to the minimum rights afforded by the various laws (and the individual contract of employment).

Since the existence of an employment relationship grants the employee many minimum rights, employers have sought to stipulate in agreements that the relationship between the parties will not be considered an employment relationship. A contractual provision to the effect that the relationship between the parties is not an employment relationship is not conclusive, and the determination that an employment relationship exists depends on the facts and circumstances of the relationship (see also Section 8 below).

2.2. WRITTEN EMPLOYMENT CONTRACTS

As noted, there is no general legislative requirement that a written contract of employment will be put in place in all cases of employment and, therefore, there is no one general legislative requirement determining the constituent elements of such a contract.

The only written document, which the employer is required to provide at the outset, is the written notification of certain terms of the employment. This written notice should include: the date of commencement of employment, the period of employment (whether for fixed period or not), a description of the employee's main duties, the identity of the employee's direct supervisor, the payments to be made to the employee, the working hours, the employee's weekly day off, the social benefits, and so on. This notice is to be provided within thirty days of the date of commencement of employment and criminal liability is imposed for failure to provide such notice (the penalty is a fine). The Notification to an Employee and Job Candidate (Terms of Employment and Screening and Recruitment Process) Law 2002 was amended in 2011 to clarify that where the employment relationship is regulated by an employment agreement containing all the elements required by the written notice and such agreement is provided within the thirty-day time frame under the law, the requirements of the law are deemed to have been met. This amendment also provides for statutory compensation in cases where the employer knowingly violates the provisions of the law, even if the employee suffered no financial loss or damage. The amount of such compensation is not to exceed NIS 15,000 unless there are special reasons, which the court must specify.

The law further imposes an obligation to provide the employee with written notification of certain changes to the terms of employment.

2.3. ORAL CONTRACTS

Legally binding employment contracts can be concluded orally under Israeli employment law, although the written notice mentioned in Section 2.2 above is still required. These contracts may be concluded from oral communications or from the conduct of the parties. In principle, employees' contractual rights can arise from employment practices at the workplace. All of these arrangements are subject to the minimum requirements of the law and the written notice requirement as aforesaid.

2.4. Employee Handbooks

Employee handbooks, as such, are not compulsory in Israel and nor are they common among purely local employers. However, there are certain aspects of employment law, in respect of which the employers are required to provide notices and information for complaints processes (e.g., the area of sexual harassment, please see further at sections 17.4 and 27 below and also employee outsourcing, please see further at Section 8.4 below).

There are some Israeli employers which form part of a larger multinational employer organization, which have adopted the handbook and policies of the overseas parent organization. These handbooks are checked against the myriad of Israeli employment laws to see that there is nothing in violation of the local Israeli laws.

2.5. Job Descriptions

A job description (of the employee's main duties) is required to be included in the notice to be provided to the employee pursuant to the Notification to an Employee and Job Candidate (Terms of Employment and Screening and Recruitment Process) Law 2002.

Where there is a written contract of employment, it would not be unusual for a job description to be included in such contract.

2.6. Offer Letters

Offer letters are sometimes provided to employees and may either contain the terms and conditions of the employment (without the need for a more detailed contract being drawn up) or may be conditional upon a detailed contract of employment.

Unless the offer letter already contains the same, in any event (and as already noted above in sections 2.1 and 2.2), the employer should provide the employee with the written notice pursuant to the Notification to an Employee and Job Candidate (Terms of Employment and Screening and Recruitment Process) Law 2002.

Where an offer letter is provided, the basic principles of offer and acceptance, as contained in the Israeli contracts law, will apply. The general principle contained in section 3(a) of the Contracts (General Part) Law 1973, is that an offeror (which would include an employer) may withdraw an offer at any time provided that there has been no acceptance of the offer prior to the time of withdrawal. Of course this is the general rule and does not address specific issues such as, for example, where the offer has stipulated that it is to be accepted within a certain period of time or within a certain manner. As far as acceptance of an offer is concerned, unless the offer requires that acceptance be provided in a certain manner, acceptance does not necessarily have to be in writing or a verbal acceptance, conduct may also constitute acceptance.

Attention should also be drawn to the principle of good faith and acting in the customary manner. By section 12 of the Contracts (General Part) Law, 1973, parties are under an obligation to negotiate contracts in good faith and in the customary manner. The Israeli Courts have commented that there is no doubt that section 12 will apply to a situation where one person, after negotiating with another, reneges on the offer for no reasonable reason, and thereby causes damage to the other party (e.g., in a case known as the *Moshe Kot* case). Section 12(b) of the Contract Law further provides that where a party has acted in violation of section 12(a), such party shall be under an obligation to compensate the other party for the damage caused to such party as a result of the negotiations (this damage would need to be proven of course by the party making the claim). Thus, if an offer is to be withdrawn, it should be done so in good faith and also accompanied by a reasonable reason, so as to seek to prevent a claim based on a breach of said section 12.

As to the method by which a withdrawal should be made, clearly such a notice should be provided to the individual in question. As to the form and content of the notice, in the absence of other legal provisions dealing specifically with this, reference can be made to section 60(a) of the Contracts (General Part) Law, 1973, which provides that notices should be made in the customary manner. It is our view that, in the employment context, the notice of the withdrawal of the offer should be made as soon as possible once withdrawal has been decided upon. It would be preferable for the notice to be made in writing and also made directly to the individual, by telephone for example.

Once an offer has been accepted, a contract has been formed between the parties, and such an offer cannot simply be withdrawn without consequences. Unless the offeror can validly justify the termination of the contract that has been formed, if the offer is withdrawn after acceptance has been given, then the general rule (assuming there were no issues concerning manner and timing of acceptance, for example) is that such withdrawal would constitute a breach of contract.

2.7. Checklist of Dos and Do Nots

– Make sure a notice pursuant to the Notification to an Employee and Job Candidate (Terms of Employment and Screening and Recruitment

Process) Law 2002 is sent to employees or, alternatively, that there is a written agreement that includes all the necessary details.
- Consider whether an offer letter is really required before sending one out.
- Check that employment terms and conditions are consistent with minimum legal requirements (e.g., as to salary, sick leave, paid leave) and any applicable collective agreements.
- Seek to have an individual employment agreement signed.
- Wherever possible, avoid entering into employment agreements for a defined or fixed term.

3. RECRUITING, INTERVIEWING, SCREENING AND HIRING EMPLOYEES

3.1. Overview

There is no one general law applicable to employee recruitment. With that in mind, it is fair to say that one of the major considerations when recruiting employees will be issues as to discrimination under, *inter alia*, the Employment Equal Opportunities Law, 1988. As mentioned in further detail in Section 17 below, this law prohibits the employer from discriminating between job applicants or employees on the following criteria: sex, sexual orientation, pregnancy, fertility treatment, parenting, age, race, religion, nationality, country of origin, political view and military reserve duty. Anything required by the character or substance of the position or job is not deemed discriminatory under the law, but the imposition of conditions that are not relevant is considered discriminatory. As noted, the prohibition against discrimination applies at all stages of employment, including at the recruitment stage.

Pursuant to a collective agreement and expansion order for the integration of persons with disabilities, employers (at least those employing more than 100 employees) will be required to employ such number of persons with disabilities as constitutes some 3% of the employer work force. A person with disabilities is defined in the Equal Rights of Handicapped Persons Law, 5748-1998. In October 2015, the follow-up committee which was established under this agreement published certain instructions with respect to the said agreement. These instructions provide, *inter alia*, that a person with disabilities for the purposes of the agreement is someone who has a disability of 40% and above, is recognized by the applicable government agency (National Insurance Institute, Ministry of Defence, Income Tax Authority, Ministry of Health) and has undergone a rehabilitation process for placement at work by one of the aforesaid government agencies; or is a veteran of the Israeli Defence Forces with a disability who has undergone a rehabilitation process for placement at work by the Ministry of Defence.

The 1998 Law requires that employers will ensure that persons with disabilities will be adequately represented among their employees. Essentially, the Expansion Order lays down the criteria for what will constitute such 'adequate representation'. An employer in respect of which, within two years of the date the Expansion Order entered into force, 3% of its work force comprises persons with disabilities will be regarded as an employee body with adequate representation for the purposes of the 1998 Law. There are certain exceptions to the application of the Expansion Order. The Expansion Order also requires the employer to appoint a person who will be responsible for the employment of persons with disabilities so as to give effect to the Expansion Order and to advance adequate representation and ensure good and proper integration of those with disabilities into the work force. It should be added that, according to the instructions published by the follow-up committee, provided the employer has taken certain actions for employment positions, the employer will be regarded as having complied with its obligations under the agreement even if it fails to meet the 3% quota mentioned above. In addition to the person to be appointed as mentioned above, these actions include maintaining written reports of the reasons for not employing individuals with disabilities.

Again it is important to recall that one of the general principles of Israeli contracts laws requires that the parties will negotiate (as well as perform and terminate) agreements in good faith and in the customary manner. This means that – *inter alia* – each party should disclose to the other party relevant information, even such information that the other party could have determined on its own. In addition to disclosure of the terms and conditions of employment, the employer is required to disclose negative aspects of the employment. The prospective employee should disclose all known limitations (non-competition, restrictions on use of confidential information, non-solicitation, etc.), previous places of employment, and the circumstances under which such prospective employee left previous employments.

3.2. Recruiting

In Israel, employers use a variety of recruiting methods. Whatever the recruitment method used – it is important to avoid unfair discrimination from the outset of the recruitment process.

The Employment Equal Opportunities Law, 1988, provides that an advertisement offering employment or referral to vocational training must use both the masculine and the feminine gender, and may not contain anything that constitutes discrimination.

In addition, consideration might need to be given to issues of privacy (see further Section 22 below).

Another aspect, which an employer may need to take into account in the recruitment process where the employer has 'head hunted' a particular potential employee from a different employer, concerns interference with contractual relationships. While the resignation by an employee from an employment agreement would not generally constitute a breach of contract, the employment agreement in question may contain certain terms and conditions which survive such resignation (such as, non-compete and non-solicitation provisions). These provisions, if breached, may in some extreme cases give rise to a possible cause of action by the former employer. Section 62(a) of the Tort Ordinance [New Version] provides that a person who knowingly and without sufficient justification causes any other person to breach a legally binding contract with a third person commits a civil wrong towards such third person. In order for an action to be founded under section 62(a), the third party will have to have suffered pecuniary damage from the interference with the contract (e.g., the former employer may have invested in the particular employee shortly before he or she was head hunted on the basis that he or she would remain and perhaps be promoted or the like).

3.3. Employment Applications

Employment applications may also be handled in a variety of methods – whether through use of application forms or not. Depending on the position in respect of which recruitment is made, the employer may request that the applicant provide a curriculum vitae and/or references.

While there is no formal requirement that applications and invitations to apply for employment be made in the local language, there is a possibility that insistence that they be made in a foreign language for all employment positions irrespective of whether the use of such foreign language arises from the nature or substance of the position or office in question, could give rise to issues under anti-discrimination laws.

The manner in which employment applications are handled may also give rise to issues under privacy laws in Israel. Further information regarding this is provided in Section 22 below. At this stage, suffice it to say that – under the Protection of Privacy Law, 1981 – the owner of a database is required to register such database in certain circumstances (depending, *inter alia*, on the amount and type of information contained in the database) and written consent from the person providing the information may be required.

Note also that, in the case of multinational employers, the transfer of information outside of Israel is be regulated by the Protection of Privacy (Transfer of Information to Databases outside the Borders of Israel) Regulations 2001.

3.4. Pre-employment Inquiries

Israeli law does not impose specific limitations on employers with respect to pre-employment inquiries. However, any investigation is subject to general limitations, such as the prohibition against discrimination (under the Employment (Equal Opportunities) Law, 1988). This law provides that the burden to prove that there was no discrimination will lie with the employer if the employer demanded information with respect to one of the protected statuses. In addition, potential information providers are restricted by specific and general rules of privacy, for instance, according to the Protection of Privacy Law, 1981 (see further below with respect to privacy protection and recruitment). In addition, where a candidate's consent is required, such consent should be explicit, informed and based on full disclosure and transparency by the employer or the recruitment agency being used. Moreover, where personal data of a candidate is being collected and processed, the collection and processing of the same needs to meet the proportionality and legitimate purpose principles.

Pursuant to the Basic Law: Human Dignity and Liberty, an employer may not oblige an employee to undergo a medical test. As a rule, invasive tests raise many legal issues and limitations. Having said that, if a medical test is required for a justified purpose, it may be required as part of the recruitment process.

The Genetic Data Law, 2000, prohibits requiring genetic data (DNA samples) from employees or applicants, unless the Minister of Health permits the demand of the genetic data.

Subject to the applicant's consent, a polygraph test is not prohibited by law, provided that the test measures relevant information. However, the Labour Courts have made comments doubting the legality of such tests.

The Employment Equal Opportunities Law 1988, forbids employers to ask applicants (or employees) for their military profile, and prohibits the use of the military profile, where it has been obtained by the employer.

Note can also be made of the following:

(a) Criminal records – the only person who can access a criminal record for the purposes of pre-employment inquiries is the individual involved. In general terms, the potential employer cannot require the applicant to produce his or her criminal record or a certificate issued by the Israeli police confirming no criminal record.

(b) Education records – the applicant can be required to provide such information – please note that the applicant can obtain certified copies issued by the relevant educational institution of his/her courses and grades.

(c) Past employment details – the applicant can be required to provide such information.

In general, it has to be recalled that, whatever information is collated during the recruitment process, careful use of the same has to be made in order to prevent issues of discrimination arising as between potential applicants.

The Protection of Privacy Law, 1981 imposes restrictions relevant to the conduct of background checks and contains data protection provisions. The type of information collected on applicants would most likely require the registration of a database. The applicant's consent would be required in order to conduct background checks and for storing, using and transferring the data. Even with consent, the information collected must be relevant, used for a legitimate business purpose and the infringement of privacy proportionate. If the employer intends to keep the data after the decision on hiring the individual is reached (with respect to hired employees and applicants that were not hired) employer will have to state the purpose of retaining such data and specific consent is required.

3.5. Pre-employment Tests and Examinations

Some employers in Israel use skill testing, in order to seek to select the applicants best suitable to fit the requirements of the employment in question as well as to establish whether these applicants have the skills and qualifications they have said they have. The Israeli case law has recognized the right of an employer to use 'suitability tests' for the purpose of choosing employees. These tests must measure the relevant traits and be reasonably reliable. The employer is not permitted to discriminate between candidates when establishing the tests.

Graphology testing is permitted, even though its reliability has been questioned, and it has been characterized as problematic because of serious interference with the candidate's rights of privacy.

As to medical testing and the like – please see Section 3.4 above.

3.6. Background, Reference and Credit Checks

Israeli law does not impose specific limitations on employers with respect to the examination of employment references. However, any examination is subject to general limitations, such as the prohibition against discrimination (under the Employment (Equal Opportunities) Law, 1988). In addition, potential information providers are restricted by specific and general rules of privacy, for instance, according to the Protection of Privacy Law, 1981.

3.7. Interviewing

As already noted, the main issue in interviewing is to ensure that the persons involved in the interview process will avoid unfair discrimination and the appearance of unfair discrimination.

It would make good practice to seek to ensure that one of the persons from the employer involved in the interview process will provide a written record of the interview and the questions asked of the candidate employees and responses given together with the interviewer's or interviewers' assessment of such candidate.

It is also possible to arrange for a follow-up interview procedure, where a large group of candidate employees has been narrowed down to a smaller group.

3.8. Hiring Procedures

As previously indicated, the employer is obliged to provide the successful applicant with a notice containing the details of his employment pursuant to the Notification Law. This is to be presented to the new employee, within thirty days of commencement of employment.

A detailed written contract of employment may also be presented (as well as or in lieu of the written notice – see Section 2.2 above) and any formal handbooks or policies and all other notifications as required by law should also be given or indicated to the employee.

The employer should also attend to all administrative matters – for example, managers' insurance funds and continuing education funds (if provided), vehicle, mobile phone, and so on.

A further amendment to the Notification Law has entered into force. This latest amendment imposes additional obligations on the employer in terms of updating a candidate employee on the employment application process. The employer is now required to update the candidate in writing at least once every two months on the progress of the employment application. In addition, the employer is now required to notify the candidate if he or she has not been accepted as an employee. This latter notice should be sent no more than fourteen days from the date on which another person is accepted to the same employment in respect of which the employment application process was conducted. There are certain exceptions to this obligation (those in the catering business, employment of up to three days, employers who employ no more than twenty-five employees, etc).

3.9. Fines and Penalties

The Labour Court has exclusive jurisdiction over all civil cases claiming a violation of the Employment (Equal Opportunities) Law, 1988. A violation of this law also results in criminal sanctions. The Court is empowered to award damages – although if no economic damage is caused – the Court is empowered to award damages of up to a certain sum without the need for proof of damage. The Court can also order mandatory injunctions or specific performance if it considers that an award of damages alone is not justified. In considering whether to make such an order, the Court is required to take into account certain factors (e.g., the effect on the relationships at the place of work and the chances that another employee would be affected as well as any applicable collective agreement).

Note should also be made of the Enforcement Law 2012, which imposes criminal and civil sanctions for violations of laws addressing recruitment issues (such as the Employment (Equal Opportunities) Law, 1988, the Genetic Information Law, 2000, etc).

3.10. Checklist of Dos and Do Nots

(a) Employers should ensure that the recruitment process does not unfairly discriminate against applicants.
(b) Where applicable employers should ensure the provisions of the Expansion Order 2014 are met with respect to the adequate representation of persons with disabilities in the work force.
(c) Pre-employment inquiries and tests should have as their aim the assessment of the suitability of the applicant for the position in question and all such inquiries and test should be performed so as to avoid the appearance of unfair discrimination.
(d) Employers should ensure that candidate consents to background checks meet all the principles applicable to such consent.
(e) Employers should not ask for military health profile.
(f) Employers should not ask for criminal record certificate.

(g) Employers are advised to document the process
(h) Employers should ensure that all notifications are sent to employees and candidate employees as required under the Notification Law.

4. MANAGING PERFORMANCE/CONDUCT

4.1. Overview

The employer's authority to manage the employees' performance and conduct derives from general principles rather than being set forth in express legislation. This authority is limited to aspects of the employees' work – acts or omissions which are work related – and, as a general rule, does not extend to the private life of the employee.

Note also, by way of a general comment, that Israeli law prohibits a third party from listening to or recording communications without the consent of at least one of the parties to the conversation. Having said that, it is possible for one of the participants in a conversation to record that conversation without the knowledge of the others. With respect to making video recordings in the workplace, the court has acknowledged that the employer might utilize video recordings for justified purposes (such as preventing shoplifting). The court mentioned that secretly videotaping employees in their workplace might constitute a violation of their rights under the Protection of Privacy Law, 1981. Even with employee consent, videotaping employees must be done for a legitimate business purpose and must be done proportionately.

Mention should also be made of the decision of the National Labour Court from early 2011 concerning the employer's right to access an employee's e-mail – this is detailed at Section 22.1 below; and also to the use of CCTV cameras in the workplace – see further at Section ___ below.

4.2. Coaching and Counselling

With the exception of requirements for position-specific training or coaching, Israel does not mandate employment-related training or coaching for employees or managers.

It might be noted that within the Ministry of Economy and Industry, there is a department for Manpower Training and Development, which assists industrial companies to train employees in different disciplines and professions.

4.3. Written Evaluations

There is no obligation for an employer to keep written evaluations on employees. However, it can be good practice to conduct meetings (including also meetings with employees whenever possible) and keep notes on an employee's performance. These notes should include all aspects and not only focus on employee's positive conduct but also indicate areas of room for improvement.

As noted in this Handbook, in most cases, before the employer can dismiss an employee, a hearing should be conducted at which the employee will have a chance to present his or her position. The existence of some form of written evaluation, which has been maintained throughout the employment period, may assist the employer is demonstrating that it has monitored the employee's performance while dismissal is under consideration.

4.4. Warnings and Suspensions

It is only possible to suspend employees in accordance with a legal source empowering the employer to suspend the employee and also for legitimate reasons. Thus, suspensions are not common in the private sector but are more common in the public sector. By way of an example, an employee's suspension was not upheld in a case where the employee refused to take a polygraph test in relation to allegations made by the employer. As a general rule, suspensions are made in cases where an employee has been indicted of a criminal offence or is subject to a criminal investigation or in cases of felony where the felony constitutes a serious moral breach which affects the ability of the employee in his employment.

Suspensions should be made by the person within the employer who is authorized to suspend employees and should only be made after careful consideration and should be proportionate to the circumstances against which it is being imposed. It is possible that the salary may be decreased for a specified period of suspension; however, this is only allowed where it is specifically regulated in an applicable collective agreement or in the individual employment agreement.

Before a decision is made to suspend an employee, the latter should be given a hearing. The hearing can be oral or in writing, provided the employee is given information prior thereto regarding the facts or allegations put against him or her.

4.5. Checklist of Dos and Do Nots

(a) Any standards for conduct and performance should be objective, non-discriminatory and clear for employees.
(b) Performance evaluations should also be objective and fair and should take into account employee input.
(c) Any warnings for improvement should specify aims or goals to be achieved.
(d) Document all such warnings and discussions.
(e) Make sure all those involved in the employee decision-making process are aware of all procedures so they will comply with them.
(f) Check carefully before choosing to suspend an employee.
(g) Conduct a hearing prior to suspension and ensure that a definitive decision is not reached prior to the hearing.

5. TERMINATION OF EMPLOYEES FOR PERFORMANCE OR DISCIPLINARY REASONS

5.1. Overview

Labour relations are deemed different from other commercial or business relations in that in the employment relationship the principle of good faith and customary manner is considered to be enhanced. This principle provides that all decisions to terminate the employment relationship should be based on relevant considerations. Accordingly, the act of dismissal must be performed in good faith and in the accepted manner, and has to be concluded on the basis of a just cause rather than arbitrary considerations. The case law has held that relevant considerations include matters such as the degree of professionalism, commitment towards the work, discipline and interpersonal skills (especially in the case of senior management).

When considering termination of employment agreements the employer should also take into consideration restrictions on the ability to terminate the employment relationship, such as:

(a) Women Labour Law 1954 – this Law forbids, *inter alia*, the dismissal of an employee due to pregnancy, during maternity leave, or during pregnancy. For the period of sixty days (at least) after maternity leave, termination is not allowed without a permit. It applies even if the employer was not aware of the pregnancy on the day of notice or on the day on which the contemplated termination should have taken effect. It should be noted that requiring the mother to stay at home until they give birth while being paid full pay – this may be regarded as a form of anticipatory termination and in effect in violation of the requirement that a permit is required during the period of at least sixty days after maternity leave. The law prohibits the dismissal of an employee undergoing fertility treatments and IVF procedures without a permit.

(b) Non-discrimination – under the Employment (Equal Opportunities) Law, 1988. Note also that, in the first case to be decided under the Equal Rights for People with Disabilities Law 1998, the District Labour Court in Jerusalem determined that the duty to ensure proper representation of persons with disabilities under that law includes giving priority to such persons over other similarly qualified employees when selecting for redundancy.

(c) The Discharged Soldiers (Reinstatement in Employment) Law, 1949, an employer may not dismiss an employee due to reserve duty and during such service. If the duty is longer than two days, dismissal is allowed only thirty days after the completion of the reserve duty, unless a permit has been obtained.

In addition to these more general considerations, there are certain requirements as the hearing process and notice to be given:

(a) *The Hearing Process* - The general rule is that employers are required to give the employee the chance to be 'heard' before termination of the employment agreement. This means that the employee has the right to be invited and heard before a decision to terminate the employment agreement is taken. The invitation should state the reasons for considering the termination in enough detail to allow the employee to effectively prepare for presenting his or her arguments at the hearing. At the hearing, the employer should clearly state the reasons underlying the considered termination. The employer is under a duty to disclose to the employee the information in the employer's possession that relates to the employee, and especially any negative information that may have an effect on the decision to terminate the employment agreement. The employer should prepare reasonably accurate minutes of the hearing.

In order for the hearing to be effective, the employer should listen unprejudiced and openly to what the employee has to say. The hearing should not be a mere technical ceremony, but rather a fair and open opportunity for the employee to convince the employer not to terminate the employment agreement.

After the employer has considered the employee's response to the claims that were raised by the employer, the employer should provide the employee with a written decision.

(b) *Notice Requirements* - Under the Advance Notice for Dismissal and Resignation Law, 2001, the employer is required to provide the employee with prior written notice of dismissal (this may not be applicable in extreme cases of termination of the employment agreement for disciplinary reasons). This Law provides that the minimum advance notice period ranges from one day to thirty days prior to the effective date of termination, depending on the length of time the employee has been with the employer. After the first year of employment, the statutory notice period is one month. If the employment agreement provides for a longer notice period than that due by the Law, the provisions of the employment agreement will prevail.

The notice of dismissal should be in writing and should specify whether the employer wishes the employee to continue to work during the notice period or not. The employer may waive this requirement, but still has to pay the salary/wages and social benefits that the employee would normally have been paid if the employee had continued working during the notice period (i.e., payment will be made during the notice period as if the employee had worked). The employer may elect to terminate the employment in such a manner that it takes immediate effect provided that the employer pays the employee the salary (but not social benefits) due for the notice period in one lump sum immediately.

The Law also provides that the employer shall give the employee a written certificate confirming the commencement and cessation dates of the employment.

5.2. Separation/Severance Pay

Issues concerning severance pay are governed primarily by the Severance Pay Law, 1963.

The Severance Pay Law lays down the minimum legal requirements as to severance pay – when it is due and how much should be paid. The employment agreement and/or an applicable collective agreement may provide terms more favourable for the employee and in addition to his or her rights under the law.

The general statutory severance pay rule under the Severance Pay Law is that an employee who has worked for at least one year continuously with the same employer or in the same place of work and whose employment is terminated by the employer is entitled to receive severance pay. The Severance Pay Law further provides that dismissal close to the expiry of the initial one year period will, unless it is proven otherwise, be considered an attempt to avoid paying severance pay, in which case severance pay will be due.

Under this general statutory severance rule, severance pay is payable in virtually every situation except voluntary resignation of the employee. Thus severance pay is payable in situations, including, amongst others, retirement, death, liquidation, or closing down of the employer.

An employee will be regarded as dismissed for the purposes of the general statutory severance pay rule in cases of both actual and constructive dismissal (e.g., where an employee resigns pursuant to a material adverse change in his or her terms or conditions of employment).

As a general rule, the amount of severance pay due is one month's salary for each year of employment and a pro rata portion for part of a year. In general terms, the last salary of the employee is taken as the basis for calculating severance pay. When determining the component elements of the salary for the purposes of the calculation of the severance pay, in addition to the base salary, some non-discretionary benefits may also be taken into account (e.g., commissions, certain non-discretionary bonuses and the like).

Employers often fund the contingent liability of paying severance pay by paying 8.33% (one-twelfth) of each payment of salary into a fund. However, if the amount of money in the fund does not cover the employer's liability for severance pay (primarily due to raises that the employee has received over the period of employment), the employer will have to pay the employee the difference, unless the employer complies with certain conditions set forth in the law.

In some industries and work places, although not required under the general statutory severance pay rule, it is customary for the employer to transfer the fund to the employee even if the employee resigns voluntarily and severance pay is not strictly required to be paid as a matter of the Severance Pay Law. If established, such a custom may be considered part of the employee's terms and conditions of employment, and the employer may, therefore, be obliged to comply with the custom.

An alternative arrangement that can be adopted is known as a section 14 arrangement. Subject to certain conditions being satisfied, a section 14 arrangement permits the employer and employee to agree that funds which have been deposited towards severance pay in the framework of management insurance or pension fund arrangement, which insurance or pension fund includes certain components, will be in lieu of the statutory severance pay. Where this section 14 arrangement applies, it would be in lieu of the usual requirement to meet any shortfall between the amount in the fund or insurance and the statutory amount required to be paid. Such a shortfall can arise where there has been employment over a number of years, accompanied by salary increases. The main condition to the application of a section 14 arrangement is the agreement that the employee shall be entitled to the amounts accrued even if he resigns, and not only when terminated by the employer, as under the general statutory severance pay rule.

In 2008, the General Collective Agreement (Framework) for Comprehensive Pension Insurance in Israel entered into effect. This Collective Agreement was extended by an Extension Order and is applicable to all the employers and employees in Israel (men – from age 21, women – from age 20), unless they are subject to a pension and severance arrangement that is more favourable to the employee. As part of this Collective Agreement (as Extended), the employer is obliged to disburse to the pension fund or management insurance on account of the employee's severance pay a certain percentage – 6% of the Insured Income. The Insured Income is the lower of the employee's salary or the average salary in Israel. This 6% is subject to arrangements under section 14 of the Severance Pay Law. This does not address the pension rules, which are addressed in section 11.3 below.

As noted above, the rules under the Collective Agreement (as Extended) do not apply where there is an arrangement in place that is more favourable to the employee. The authorities are of the view that where an employer funds the contingent liability of paying severance pay by paying 8.33% (1/12) of each payment of salary into a management insurance or pension fund, the same will be regarded as an arrangement which is more favourable to the employee, and the provisions of Collective Agreement (as Extended) with respect to severance pay will not then be applicable. But also see further in section 11.3 below regarding the pension rules.

In addition, certain sectors may be subject to other rules. For instance, industry employees are subject to the Industrial Sector Extension Order – Framework for Comprehensive Pension Insurance in Industry, 2006.

Where the employer has paid contributions to a management insurance or pension fund, the employee will require a letter from the employer confirming the termination of the employment in order that the employee will be able to withdraw funds from the insurance or pension fund.

Also, upon termination, the employer is required to compensate the employee for accrued and unused vacation days and other accrued pay (such as convalescence pay – dmei havra'a).

Upon termination, it is advisable (though not always possible) to have the employee sign a letter of release and waiver. This waiver should contain a detailed list of the entitlements and amounts due and payable to the employee upon the termination. These entitlements cannot be conditioned upon the employee signing the letter of waiver and will have to be paid whether or not the same is signed by the employee. However, monetary or other benefits provided to the employee in excess of his or her entitlements, and on an ex-gratia basis, may be conditional upon his or her signature on a waiver. It would make sense to suggest to the employee that he or she may take independent legal advice before signing and to record such fact in the letter.

5.3. Fines and Penalties

The law prescribes the time for payment of severance pay and imposes an obligation of punitive damages (calculated as a percentage of the severance pay) for delayed payment.

The penalties imposed on employers who breach their obligations to act in good faith and/or to conduct a proper hearing and the like are usually monetary. Nevertheless, there is also the possibility that, in certain cases, the labour courts would determine that an unlawful dismissal is null and void, and would, therefore, require reinstatement.

Please also note that liability may also be imposed under the Enforcement Law 2011 for failure to comply with all the statutory obligations that are relevant to termination.

5.4. Checklist of Dos and Do Nots

- Always recall that, as with other aspects of the employment agreement, termination is also required to be performed in good faith.
- Make sure that all the procedures are adopted – the employee is given a hearing before the decision on the termination of the employment agreement and all notices are provided.
- Make sure the liability for severance pay payments is covered, whether through management insurance or otherwise.
- Do not terminate an employment agreement close to the expiration of the first year anticipating no severance pay liability.
- Take into account that certain employees may not be terminated for certain periods, for instance during pregnancy, maternity leave, military reserve duty, and so on.
- Make sure all severance pay liability is paid on time to prevent high penalty payments being incurred.
- Check all payments due and owing to the employee upon termination.
- If feasible, have employee sign off on letter of waiver. For basic entitlements, this cannot be a condition to employees receiving payments.

6. LAY-OFFS, REDUCTIONS IN FORCE AND/OR REDUNDANCIES AS A RESULT OF JOB ELIMINATIONS OR OTHER RESTRUCTURING

6.1. Overview

The general considerations set forth in section 5.1 above apply also to termination during lay-offs, reductions in work force, redundancies and other restructuring.

As already mentioned in Section 5.1 above, employers – as a general rule – should give the employee the chance to be 'heard' before termination of the employment agreement. This means that the employee has the right to be invited and heard before a decision to terminate the employment agreement is taken.

Accordingly, also in cases where the employer is considering the termination of the employment for any reason – downsizing, restructuring and the like – the employer should approach the employee, in writing, and invite the employee to a hearing before the decision is made.

The requirements of the Advance Notice for Dismissal and Resignation Law, 2001, as detailed in section 5.1 above, and the Severance Pay obligation detailed in Section 5.2 above, are likewise relevant to lay-offs, reductions in work force, redundancies and other restructuring.

Pursuant to the Employment Service Law, 1959, an employer which delivers notices of dismissal to ten or more employees is required to notify the Employment Service Bureau.

6.2. Restrictions in Force/Layoffs/Job Eliminations

The restrictions noted with respect to termination of employment for performance or disciplinary reasons in section 5.1 apply also to terminations due to force/layoffs/job eliminations.

In addition to the points noted in the Overview above, also in cases of reductions in force/layoffs/job eliminations, the employer is required to compensate the employee for accrued and unused vacation days and other accrued pay (such as convalescence pay – dmei havra'a). Depending on the type of compensation, the redemption might be calculated in accordance with the level of salary being paid to the terminated employee at the time of termination.

In addition, in these cases, the employee may well come and request a recommendation or referral letter from the employer.

It is also advisable (if not always possible) to seek to have the employee sign a letter of release and waiver (see further at section 5.2 above).

6.3. Fines and Penalties

See Section 5.3 above on fines and penalties.

6.4. Checklist of Dos and Do Nots

- See Section 5.4 above.
- If required, ensure that notice is provided to the Employment Service Bureau when necessary.

7. LABOUR AND EMPLOYMENT LAW RAMIFICATIONS UPON ACQUISITION OR SALE OF A BUSINESS

7.1. Overview

In general terms, the acquisition or sale of a business may follow one of two main structures – share acquisition or asset acquisition:

Share Acquisition– Where the acquisition or sale of a business is via a sale or acquisition of the shares of a business, this gives rise to fewer concerns under Israeli employment laws – the business entity in this case will remain the same and the employer will remain the same. However, in such cases, it makes sense – and is generally is a good idea – to inform and communicate with the work force about the sale/acquisition process in order to allay concerns and fears. In some cases, even a share transaction may be regarded as a change in the employment terms, which could give the employees the right to resign and receive severance pay. Likewise, any reorganization in the existing work force (lay-offs, redundancies, etc.) by the new owner would be subject to the general principles outlined above in Section 6.

Asset Acquisition– In an asset acquisition or sale, the considerations may be different. In such a transaction, the former employment relationship is terminated and all of the employees or some of them are hired by the new employer. The selling entity is obliged to pay the employees that are not hired by the new employer (employees that were not offered a position by the new employer and employees that refused such an offer) all rights upon termination. The parties to the transaction can deal with the selling entity's obligations towards the transferring employees in in one of two ways: (i) cashing out of employee rights; or (ii) assumption of existing employee rights by new employer.

Furthermore, in any event (including in a share acquisition where there is no change of the employer legal entity), prior to the occurrence of any significant change in the employment terms or upon a contemplated change of ownership in a workplace where the employees are unionized, the employer should (i) transfer to the employees' union all the information relevant to the employees in the framework of the contemplated transaction; (ii) consult with the employees' union concerning the best way in which to safeguard their interests (such consultation should be frank and straightforward, and the employer should be open to hear the employees' union stands and concerns); and (iii) negotiate with the employees' union in order to reach an agreement that would protect the employees' rights after the completion of the contemplated transaction.

7.2. Acquisition of a Business

As mentioned above, in the case of a business asset acquisition, employees may be transferred in one of two ways: (i) cashing out of employee rights; or (ii) assumption of existing employee rights by new employer.

Clearly, whatever way is used, it is necessary to conduct a thorough due diligence (legal and accounting) with respect to all payments which may be due to the employees upon termination of the previous employment and to ensure that all these payments are fully and properly handled in accordance with the manner selected for the transaction in question.

Termination and Rehiring

When this method is chosen, the selling entity will pay the employees all the payments that they are entitled to receive upon termination. This includes, amongst others, accrued vacation days, dmei havra'a, payment in lieu of prior notice (if notification of the termination of employment was not given in a timely manner, including in cases where the selling entity chooses to keep the fact of a pending sale confidential until a late stage, such that requisite prior notice cannot be given) and is especially important for severance pay purposes. If the selling entity pays the severance pay upon termination of employment by the selling entity, the purchasing entity will not be liable for the severance pay due for the period of employment with the selling entity prior to the asset acquisition.

Please note that even when the parties choose to cash out the employee rights, the seniority of the employees with the selling entity does influence the employee rights with the purchasing entity. This is due to the fact that the employment period with the purchasing entity is considered to be 'at the same work place' as the employment with the selling entity. Such seniority will be taken into account, for instance, for purposes of determining the number of minimal vacation days, dmei havra'a, sick days due under the relevant laws.

Assumption of Employees with Continuity of Employment

By means of this alternative, the acquirer will simply take over the obligations of the selling entity towards the transferring employees with all outstanding liabilities and dues and there will be no payment of severance payments or other rights by the selling entity. In this situation, the purchasing entity may be exposed to future liabilities towards the transferred employees. For example, there may be liabilities not covered by the funds put to one side for severance pay under management insurance or severance pay funds (e.g., accrued vacation days, increases in salary over a number of years, etc.). Therefore, the new owner and employer should take into consideration any such existing exposure.

Please note that it is not possible to force the employees to accept the employment offer of the purchasing entity and they may still elect to resign and claim the severance pay package.

The approval of the Income Tax Authority is required in advance in order to transfer the employee pension funds and managers insurance from the selling entity to the purchasing entity. The request for such approval must be submitted at least sixty days in advance.

7.3. Acquisition Checklist

- Make sure that the seller provides full, accurate and up to date information regarding all the employees and all of their seniority and benefits as well as potential for application of any collective agreement or extension thereof.
- Receive details of accrued amounts certified by the third-party funds (pension funds, insurance companies).
- Purchaser should engage services of an accountant well-versed in the accounting side of employees and their salaries and benefits.
- Decide which form of acquisition is preferred – share or asset and adjust the representations and warranties regarding employee and employee payments accordingly.
- Make sure that all payments due and owing to employees on or before completion date for transfer of the business (shares or assets) will have been taken into account in full and letters of waiver obtained (where used).
- Make sure to have appropriate indemnification provisions in place and, if possible, collateral.
- Make sure that the transaction takes into account the time required in order to obtain the Income Tax Authority's approval for the transfer of the

employee pension funds and managers insurance and that the request is submitted well in advance of the closing date of the transaction.

7.4. Sale of a Business

In terms of the sale of a business, the considerations of the selling party are really the mirror image of those outlined in Section 7.2 above regarding the acquiring party.

7.5. Sale of a Business Checklist

In terms of the sale of a business, the checklist of the selling party is really the mirror image of those outlined in Section 7.3 above regarding the acquiring party.

8. USE OF ALTERNATIVE WORKFORCES: INDEPENDENT CONTRACTORS, CONTRACT EMPLOYEES AND TEMPORARY OR LEASED WORKERS

8.1. Overview

There is no specific legislation in Israel which defines the distinction between employees on the one hand, and independent contractors on the other. This distinction has been left to the courts to determine and the distinction is made based on the essence of the relationship rather than the label, which the parties choose to attribute to it. In some cases, the distinction is a fine one and the Israeli Labour Courts have tended to favour an interpretation under which the individual obtains the protection of the labour laws. This can make it difficult to evade the application of the labour laws.

There is legislation, which governs the outsourcing of employees through manpower contractors – the Employment of Employees by Manpower Contractors Law, 1996.

More recently, as noted above, legislation has entered into force seeking to enhance and make more efficient the enforcement of labour laws throughout the work force – see further at Section 8.4 below.

8.2. Independent Contractors

a. Definition

There is no legislative definition of what constitutes an 'independent contractor' as opposed to an 'employee', or vice versa, in Israeli law. Rather, this distinction has been left for the courts to determine. The Israeli Labour Courts have traditionally applied the 'integration test' in order to determine which side of the line a given relationship may fall. In applying the integration test, the courts will look to the substance (and circumstances) of the relationship and not to the label attributed to it by the parties.

In essence, integration test comprises two elements: (i) is the individual integrated into the organization; and (ii) do the tasks to be undertaken by such individual form an integral part of the business of the organization. If so, the individual would be regarded as an employee rather than independent contractor.

More recently, the integration test has been overtaken by a test, which requires analysing the relationship against all the circumstances of the relationship as well as the applicable laws. This test has been adopted by the labour courts and the courts will look at all factors – expenses and income, where is the risk of expense borne as against the chance of profit, intention of the parties, their behaviour, the nature of the business, the extent to and manner in which the individual is subjected to supervision by the person engaging them, the power of the person engaged to engage employees of his or her own, how payments are handled towards tax authorities, and so on.

b. Creating the Relationship

There is no formal legislative requirement that an independent contractor relationship will be created by a document in writing signed by the parties. However, it is good commercial practice to reduce the terms and conditions between the parties to writing.

c. Compensation

The compensation for independent contractors will be as per agreed between the parties and may comprise a fixed retainer and/or some form of performance-based earnings, depending on the nature of the services being provided.

The compensation will be paid on a gross basis – the person engaging the independent contractor does not make withholding tax deductions (as opposed to the case with employees, where income tax and other payments – management insurance, national health insurance, etc. are withheld at source); provided that the independent contractor has an exemption from withholding at source. Usually, the independent contractor agreement will provide that the independent contractor is receiving the compensation on a gross basis and is responsible for paying all the taxes with respect thereto.

The compensation should be paid against a VAT invoice and any other income tax authority forms as may be required, to be issued by the independent contractor to the person engaging them.

d. Other Terms and Conditions

There are certain terms and conditions, which should be taken into account when preparing an independent contractor agreement under Israeli law:

(i) Where there is a real concern that the independent contractor relationship could be interpreted as an employer-employee one, it is usual to advise that the person engaging the independent contractor will include in the agreement (assuming there is a written agreement) what has become known as a 'Gidron Clause'– in essence, this clause is intended to seek to prevent the independent contractor from seeking to claim in the future that he or she was in fact an employee of the person engaging them.

Such a clause will only be implemented if the individual was offered a post as employee, but preferred to be taken on as independent contractor and waives all rights and benefits as employee. The clause will typically regulate the situation, should it be determined (by the courts, tax authorities, etc.) that the relationship is nevertheless one of employer/employee, regarding the salary and benefits payments such that the salary will be deemed to be a certain percentage of the compensation stated (to take account of withholding deductions which are required for tax and the like). Typically, such a clause can contain an indemnity from the individual towards the engaging entity to cover such withholding payments.

It is noted that as a result of case law where the employer engages an individual as an independent contractor in cases where it is clear to the employer that such individual is an employee, and the relationship is later determined to be one of employer-employee, then the total monthly compensation paid to the individual will be the base for calculating the social benefits retroactively. In cases where this is not clear, the employee (formerly independent contractor) will not be entitled to additional amounts over that such individual received as an independent contractor, where the compensation received as an independent contractor is more than the salary that the individual would have received as an employee, plus the employer's cost of social benefits. It was also determined that in any case, the individual that was later recognized as an employee will not reimburse the employer.

(ii) Similarly in the case as per (i) above, it is usual to include a tax indemnity in case the situation is interpreted to give rise to employer-employee relations.
In all independent contractor agreements, provision should be made for ownership of intellectual property rights and also for confidential treatment of information as well as return thereof upon termination or expiration of the relationship.

(iii) It might also be relevant (depending on the circumstances of the relationship) to regulate non-competition and non-solicitation on the part of the independent contractor.

(iv) Provisions as to term and termination should be included. Where the independent contractor has been paid on a performance basis, it might be necessary to regulate whether the contractor should receive payment for performance which took place before the termination but which only came to fruition after its termination.

(v) Where the independent contractor is non-Israeli, it might be necessary to give consideration to choice of law and jurisdiction provisions.

8.3. Contract Workers

Contract workers are like independent contractors or freelancers under Israeli law and there is no specific legislation addressing these types of workers. The principles as per Section 8.2 above would apply here.

In essence, the treatment of contract workers will be the same as for independent contractors. Where the relationship between the engaging person and the contract worker or freelancer is found to be an employer-employee one (using the test looking at all the circumstances of the case, mentioned above), then such contract worker or freelancer could be considered as an employee entitled to all the minimum rights and benefits offered to employees under Israeli law.

8.4. Leased Workers

Issues concerning leased workers are primarily governed by the Employment of Employees by Manpower Contractors Law, 1996. This law governs the operations of manpower contractors. A manpower contractor is defined in this law as a person engaged in the provision of manpower services by its employees for the purposes of work for another person and also a private bureau (as defined under the Employment Services Law, 1957) engaged in the provision of manpower services. A private bureau is one engaged in the brokering of employment – arranging meetings between those seeking employment and those seeking employees.

The Law requires that a manpower contractor will hold a license, issued by the Minister of Labour and Social Affairs pursuant to that law. The law also lays down the conditions for the grant of such a license (at least three years' experience, provision of a bank guarantee or other suitable surety for the fulfilment of obligations towards its employees, has no prior convictions for a flagrantly dishonourable offence or of an offence which makes it unfit to act as a manpower contractor). Where a manpower contractor wishes to provide manpower services of employees who are not Israeli residents or of employees from Israel to a workplace abroad, a special license is required.

By contrast with the general requirement under Israeli labour laws, the employment agreement for employees of a manpower contractor is required to be in writing (unless a collective agreement that prescribes the employment conditions of the manpower contractor's employees applies to them).

The law provides that where the employee of the manpower contractor is employed with the party ordering the employment services for a period exceeding nine continuous months, such employee shall be deemed to be an employee of the party ordering the employment services. In such event, the period of service seniority acquired by the employee during the period of his employment by the manpower contractor for the party ordering the employment services (the first nine months) shall be added to the period of service seniority thereafter, with the party ordering the employment services.

In early 2004, a general collective agreement was reached between the employers' and the employees' organizations in the labour contracting sector. The purpose of this collective agreement is to protect the rights of the leased labour workforce. This agreement – through an extension order issued by the Minister of Industry Trade and Labour – applies employment rights (working hours, annual leave, travel expenses, sick leave, clothing expenses, pension arrangements, contributions to mutual funds, etc.) to all the leased labour workforce even if they are not members of the employer's organization that signed the agreement.

Note also that under the Employment Equal Opportunities Law 1988 the party ordering employment services should not discriminate between employees and candidate employees of manpower contractors.

As noted above, the Law for the Enhancement of Enforcement of Labour Laws 2011 seeks to bring about greater and more efficient enforcement of labour laws throughout the Israeli work force, with State interference in the contract between a party ordering employment services and the manpower contractor.

This Law enables the imposition of financial sanctions using administrative proceedings in addition to the imposition of criminal liability for violations of employment laws. In these proceedings, a senior supervisor, who will be appointed by the Minister of Economy and Industry, and who is defined in this Law as the 'Supervisor', will deliver a notice to a business in cases where he has reasonable grounds to believe that the employer has violated those provisions of the law, which are set forth in the Second Appendix to the 2011 Law. The employer has a right of hearing before the Supervisor. The Second Appendix to this Law divides the amount of the financial sanction between three categories of legal provisions. The financial sanction increases with the severity of the violation of the legal requirement and rates are from NIS 5,000 through to NIS 35,000 (or 50% of that amount in respect of an individual who takes on employees but not within the framework of a business, profession or public activity). It is possible to appeal against the Supervisor's decisions regarding the imposition of financial sanctions before an appeals committee. In the event that the employer regards itself as damaged by the decision of the appeals committee, the employer is entitled to appeal the same to the Local *Labour* Court. In addition, the law allows for the imposition of financial sanctions on the CEO of the employer, at a rate which is 50% of the financial sanction and after a warning has been issued by the Supervisor.

The 2011 law also provides for the imposition of the financial sanctions on the party ordering employment services. The law defines the services in respect of which it applies in this respect as services in one of the following fields: guarding and security; cleaning; meals, if the services are provided to the employees of the party ordering employment services.

A demand for payment issued under the 2011 Law to the manpower contractor will also apply directly to the party ordering employment services. However, it will not be acted on before the Supervisor has delivered the party who ordered employment services a notice and warning by terms of which such party is required to amend the violation or act in good faith to terminate the agreement with the contractor and realize the collateral which the manpower contractor provided.

In addition to the possibility of imposing financial sanctions on the party ordering employment services, in the event that certain conditions set forth in the 2011 Law are met (at least four employees – whether from one or more manpower services provider, more than six months continuous employment with the party ordering and notice of violations has been sent to the party ordering and breach has not been remedied), the obligations of the employer who is also a manpower contractor towards its employees will also apply to the party ordering employment services. These obligations will apply proportionately to the period during which the employee was actually working at the party ordering employment services. In this case, the provisions of the applicable laws (as set forth in the Third Appendix to the 2011 Law) and the provisions of applicable extension orders (including those concerning payment of annual recreation pay [dmei havra'a], reimbursement of travel expenses, pension, High Holiday pay and index linkage) will also apply to the party ordering employment services.

The party ordering employment services is required to take reasonable measures in order to try to prevent damage to the rights of the employees of the manpower contractor who are working for it (the party ordering the services). To that end, the party ordering employment services is required to find an efficient system at the work place for the delivery of notices concerning damage to rights (and investigation into the same) and to bring this system to the attention of the employees of the manpower contractor working at such work place.

The 2011 Law further provides that the party ordering employment services is required to ensure certain conditions in the agreement between it and the manpower contractor are included such as: the elements of the salary which will be paid to the manpower contractor for its employees and the cost of the minimum wage, a declaration of the manpower contractor concerning other costs including profit, the undertaking of the party ordering the service to pay an amount which is not less than the cost of the minimum wage and such additional costs (the 'Contract Conditions'). The party ordering employment services is further required to verify that the cost of the minimum salary is not less than the value of the hour's work as determined and it should verify that it is not paying the contractor a sum which is less than the hour's work which is determined for an hour's work for employees of the manpower contractor. The 2011 Law does provide the party ordering the services with defences to a civil claim where the violation has been remedied in full or in certain circumstances in which the party ordering employment services relied in good faith on periodic checks.

As well as civil liability, in those cases where the party ordering employment services did not determine Contract Conditions, as mentioned in the preceding paragraph, the 2011 Law provides for the imposition of criminal liability. If a criminal violation is committed by an entity, by virtue of the 2011 Law, the CEO will be deemed to have violated his or her obligations under the 2011 Law unless it can be proven that he or she did everything possible in order to fulfil those obligations, since the CEO is obliged under that Law to supervise and take all possible steps to prevent such violation.

The 2011 Law empowers the Supervisor to deliver the CEO a warning letter in those cases where there has been a violation of the 2011 Law. By virtue of the 2011 Law, in cases of failure to implement the measures demanded by the Supervisor, the CEO will be deemed to have violated his or her obligations to act as required in the warning unless the CEO can prove that he or she did everything possible to implement the measures.

The 2011 Law prohibits party ordering employment services to condition the rights of the employee of the manpower contractor. In addition, a provision in the agreement by terms of which an employee of the manpower contractor waived in advance his or her rights under the 2011 Law towards the party ordering the services or a provision conditioning such rights of the employee, whether express or implied, will not be valid.

The parties cannot contract out of the 2011 Law obligations. Likewise, it is not possible to insure, directly or indirectly, a person in respect of a financial sanction which may be imposed on it under the 2011 Law and any agreement to so insure will be set aside. Also, any provision in the agreement between the party ordering employment services and the manpower contractor for the indemnification of the party ordering the services or for any payment to it in respect of its obligations under the 2011 Law, is invalid.

8.5. Checklist Dos and Do Nots

(a) Do engage a reputable manpower agency and execute a written agreement with the manpower agency.
(b) In the agreement with manpower contractor make sure the Contract Conditions are included and meet the minimum requirements as per law.
(c) The party ordering employment services should make sure adequate supervisory measures are put in place as per the 2011 Law.
(d) If engaging from a manpower contractor, ensure that an efficient system at the work place for the delivery of notices concerning damage to rights (and investigation into the same) and notification of this system to the employees is put in place, as per the 2011 Law.

9. OBLIGATION TO BARGAIN COLLECTIVELY WITH TRADE UNIONS: RIGHT TO STRIKE AND A COMPANY'S RIGHT TO CONTINUE BUSINESS OPERATIONS

9.1. Overview of Unions' Right to Organize

Although constitutional rights were listed in the Basic Law: Human Dignity and Freedom and the Basic Law: Freedom of Occupation, freedom of association was not expressly mentioned in these laws. Nevertheless, freedom of association has been recognized for many years as a fundamental right by the Supreme Court and the National Labour Court. Indeed the Supreme Court and the National Labour Court have held that freedom of association is a constitutional right, derived from the right of human dignity; and National Labour Court judgments have held that the freedom to strike and join, or not join a union are part of freedom of association.

There are two focal court decisions on the employees' right of freedom of association and which strengthen the protection of the employees' right of organization during its initial phase. Both decisions concerned employees working in the telecommunications sector. The first case – the *Pelephone* Case – is set forth in section 9.2 below and for details of the second case *see* section 9.3 below.

The National Labour Court has determined that employees have the right whether or not to join a union. However, in the organized sector of the workforce (currently much lower than in the earlier years after the establishment of the State of Israel), non-members are obligated under the terms of the collective agreement to pay the union a service fee instead of union dues. Non-members are entitled to all the benefits set forth in the collective agreement.

9.2. Right of Employees to Join Unions

Under Israeli law, employees are entitled to join unions. There are a number of sections in the Collective Agreements Law 1957, which give employees certain rights regarding union membership.

Section 33H of the said Law provides that each employee has the right to act for a workers' union, to be a member of the same and to act within its framework.

Section 33I of this Law further provides that the employer will not prevent a representative of a workers' union from entering the work place where an employee is employed in order to promote the right as provided in section 33H and to promote the interests of the employees, taking into account the needs of the work.

Section 33J(a) of the Collective Agreements Law 1957, provides that an employer shall not dismiss an employee, worsen an employee's work conditions or prevent a person from being hired due to membership or activity in an employees union or committee, or due to efforts to establish an employees union or committee. The remedies for a violation of this provision will be monetary compensation to the employee and it can be awarded without actual proof of loss and the court has power to issue an injunction against dismissal.

The first case mentioned in section 9.1 above, the Pelephone Case, concerned the extent to which the employer can approach its employees during the initial phase of their organization in order to present the employer's stand with respect to such organization. The National Labour Court (whose decision was subsequently adopted by the Supreme Court) discussed in full the basic rights which are in balance during that process – the freedom of expression of the employer and it proprietary rights on the one hand and the freedom of organization of employees on the other. The Court took the view that during the initial phase of organization, and before the employees' organization has appointed a representative, there is a presumption that the presentation of the employer's position constitutes unfair pressure and influence on the employees. So, during this initial phase of organization, until the appointment of a representative union, the employees' right of organization takes precedence over the employer's freedom of expression. The National Labour Court also presented guidelines concerning the behaviour of the parties during this phase – the employer cannot offer benefits or exceptional guarantees to employees depending on whether an employee is organized in a union or not; it should not contact employees individually or set up meetings with groups of employees or hold individual conversations with them.

9.3. How Employees Select Unions

Within a work place (the definition of which can be complex) if more than a third of the employees are members of a union and no other union has more members, such union will be recognized as representing the employees. As to the definition of the work place or relevant bargaining unit for this purpose, there is some case law as to whether it encompasses the entire employer organization or individual sectors or plants within that organization.

For instance, the Hot Mobile Case, concerned the question as to what constitutes the relevant 'bargaining unit' within a corporate group set-up in the context of the employees' right to organize. In that instance, because of the structural divisions between the different companies making up the HOT group of companies and also in light of the specific permits issued to the cellular phone company within that group, the court found that such company (cellular phone) was the relevant bargaining unit for the purposes of considering the employees' right to organize and the extent to which such right had been interfered with by the employer. The court also found that the employer had carried out acts which were intended to damage the employees' right to organize, these included: trying to bring about a dispute between two employee organizations within the group; attempts to sign employees on a new employment agreement to transfer them to a different unit within the group; attempts to try to discover which employees had joined the movement to organize and which had not and to try to persuade the latter not to join. At the end of the day, a fine was imposed on the employer in respect of these activities and again – as in the Pelephone Case – the court emphasized the importance of the freedom of organization and especially during the initial phase.

9.4. Pre-election Campaigning

Pre-election campaigning is allowed at the work place.

9.5. Unfair Labour Practices

Please see Section 9.4 above.

9.6. Relocation of Work/Shutdown of Business

According to the Severance Pay Law, 1963, an employee whose employment has ceased owing to the bankruptcy of his or her employer or, where the employer is a corporation, owing to the winding-up or striking off thereof, shall be entitled to severance pay as if such employee had been dismissed.

Under the Acquisition of Undertakings by Employees (Special Cases) Law 1987, a special fund is established for the grant of loans for the acquisition of undertakings by the employees of such undertakings. An undertaking is defined as a place of employment in industry or in the building trade in which not more than 200 employees are employed and which has been closed down completely or its main industry has been discontinued for three months or which is owned by a body corporate against which a receiving order has been made or which is owned by an individual against whom a receiving order has been made. The works committee of an undertaking may apply for assistance from the fund for the purpose of acquisition of the undertaking by its employees. In order to make such an application, the works committee requires the majority approval of a meeting of the employees of the undertaking.

The application is made to a committee, established under the said Law. Once an application is received, the committee is to seek an opinion on the economic, legal and employment aspects connected with the application.

In order to acquire the undertaking, the employees are required to form a cooperative society under the Cooperative Societies Ordinance and assistance from the fund is provided as a loan to such cooperative society.

9.7. Checklist of Dos and Do Nots

- Do not take action that could be considered as interference with employees' rights to act for a workers' union, to be a member of the same and to act within its framework.
- Do not prevent a representative of a workers' union from entering the work place.
- Do not dismiss an employee, worsen an employee's work conditions or prevent a person from being hired due to membership or activity in an employees' union or committee, or due to efforts to establish an employees' union or committee.

10. WORKING CONDITIONS: HOURS OF WORK AND PAYMENT OF WAGES: BY STATUTE OR COLLECTIVE AGREEMENTS

10.1. Overview of Wage and Hours Laws

The Minimum Wages Law, 1987 provides the legal framework for the minimum wages in Israel. The Wages Protection Law 1958 prohibits deductions from wages or salaries up to a certain amount. The Israeli general law of contracts requires employers to fulfil their employment contracts and pay the wages agreed upon.

In addition, the Wages Protection Law, 1958 requires employers to pay wages on time. Unless other better conditions are set in the employment contract, the employer is required to pay monthly salaried employees within nine days of the end of the month in respect of which such employee is being paid. Failure to make such payment on time carries sanctions as indicated in the paragraph below.

The Wages Protection Law also creates a draconian remedy to ensure that wages are paid on time – for the first week of delay there is a penalty of 5%and for every week thereafter a penalty of 10%. So, for example, an employer who pays wages a month late must pay a 35% delay penalty in addition to the wage. This acts as a powerful incentive for employers to pay wages on time. Note that the Israeli Labour Courts may reduce the penalty in cases where the wage was paid late due to a bona fide mistake on the part of the employer or a disagreement between the parties as to the existence of the debt, and so on.

The Wages Protection Law further regulates the manner in which payment can be made (e.g., wages must be paid at the place of employment or into the employees' bank account).

Under the Hours of Work and Rest Law 1951, the working week is set at forty-five hours per week. However, the basic working week has been limited by orders published by the Minister and applicable to most employees, first to forty-three hours and, as from April 2018, to forty-two hours per week. This decrease in the working week (from forty-three to forty-two hours) is to be given effect by reducing one hour from one defined and fixed working day in the week, as notified to the employees by the employer. For shift work the decrease can be effected over more than one day.

Under the provisions of the Hours of Work and Rest Law 1951, as amended, applicable to night work in a plant where there is shift work it is possible to employ an employee on night work for not more than one week out of a period of two weeks.

This law also provides that the basic working day is eight hours, but in an order published by the Minister it is possible to have a basic working day of up to nine hours for employees who work a five-day working week (both subject to the one shorter day per week as noted above). There are some exceptions to the Hours of Work and Rest Law (see further Section 10.7 below). When determining whether these exceptions apply, the court will look to the substance of the employment position and not to the label the parties attribute to it and tend to interpret the exceptions narrowly.

10.2. Minimum Wage

The Minimum Wages Law provides that the minimum wage shall be 47.5% of the average wage as of 1 April each year. As at the time of writing, the minimum wage is NIS 5,300 (approximately EUR 1,266) per month.

The Minimum Wages Law provides for both criminal (fines or prison sentence) and civil liability in case of its violation (an employee may sue the employer for compensation for the difference between the actual wages and the minimum statutory wage). The implementation of the Law is attended to by the Enforcement and Regulatory Administration within the Ministry of Economy and Industry (this Administration was established in mid-2004).

This Law also requires the employer to put up a notice in the work place notifying as to the minimum wage currently in force (updating it as required) and a telephone number employees can contact at the above-mentioned Enforcement and Regulatory Administration,

The importance of employee rights in this respect has been reinforced by a Decision of the District Court of Tel-Aviv in 2008. The said court annulled a tender issued by a certain Municipality in Israel in a case where there was concern that successful company would not be able meet its obligations with respect to its employees' rights. The court was concerned that the costing of the winning bid in this case could have exposed the employees to the risk of erosion of their minimum rights under law and that there was a risk that the workers would carry the burden of the cost of deficit and not their employer.

10.3. Overtime

The Hours of Work and Rest Law, 1951 generally prohibits overtime unless a permit is obtained. There is a general permit that allows overtime and, following the change to the working week hours, the permit now provides for up to sixteen additional hours per week overtime whether the employee works a five day or six day week, with a per day maximum of twelve hours. It is also provided that where during the working week the employee is employed in night work, the length of the working week shall not exceed fifty-eight hours (including overtime).

With respect to overtime, this Law sets forth the amount of overtime to be paid: 125% for the first two hours per day and 150% thereafter. The pay for working on the weekly rest period is 150% of the regular pay in addition to time off instead of the time worked during the weekly rest period (a permit for working on the weekly rest period is required). The Wages Protection Law, 1958 prohibits the inclusion of overtime payment in the normal wage or salary and it should be dealt with separately. However, having said that, there has been a common practice especially in the hi-tech industry in Israel to make a global overtime payment. However, this practice is not the mechanism for overtime payment prescribed by the law.

Note that under the Wages Protection Law, 1958 – as amended – the burden of proof with respect to overtime where the employee is claiming payment for overtime hours of up to fifteen hours per week or sixty hours per month is on the employer. Thus the employer will be required to prove that the employee was not available to work the hours claimed by the employee in the claim for payment; unless the employer presents the register of hours as required by law (see further on this in Section 10.9 below).

As noted in Section 10.7 below, there are certain exemptions to the Hours of Work and Rest Law.

10.4. Meal and Rest Periods

Under the Hours of Work and Rest Law the employee that works six hours or more a day is entitled to at least forty-five minutes of break, including one meal break of thirty minutes. In addition, this law also entitles religious employees to short prayer breaks.

This law further provides that employees should have a thirty-six-hour weekly rest period. Employment on the rest day is prohibited unless authorized by the Minister of Labour where working is deemed in the interest of the general public due to security, safety, and economic considerations (section 12 of the Hours of Work and Rest Law).

10.5. Deductions from Wages

The Wages Protection Law also protects workers from wage deductions which have not been authorized by the worker or specifically required or allowed by law. Permitted deductions include: income taxes, union membership and agency fees, disciplinary fines agreed upon in the employment contract or in a collective agreement, and debt to the employer evidenced by employee's written undertaking which may not exceed 25% of the salary during employment and may reach the full salary after termination of employment.

10.6. Garnishment

Section 8 of the Wages Protection Law safeguards a proportion of the employee's salary from attachment, transfer or charges. The amount protected correlates to the guaranteed income, as determined in the Income Guarantee Law, 1980. The calculation of the guaranteed amount of income is fairly complex and needs to be checked carefully on a case-by-case basis. Note that in the case of child support and maintenance payments, the situation is different and the debtor does not have income guarantee.

10.7. Exemptions to Wage and Hour Laws

The Hours of Work and Rest Law exempts certain branches of the economy and employers from the application of that law. These include the police, aircrew and sailors. The most litigated exception is for 'persons employed in management positions or positions requiring a special degree of personal trust' and 'employees, the conditions and circumstances of whose employment render it impossible for the employer to supervise their work hours and hours of rest'. The interpretation of these two exceptions has become increasingly narrow.

10.8. Child Labour

Under the Youth Labour Law 1953, youth under the age of 15 years cannot be employed. Where a child has attained 15 years and is subject to compulsory education, he or she shall not be employed unless as an apprentice under the Apprenticeship Law 1953 or pursuant to a certification issued by an inspector of the Ministry of Education and Culture.

Note though that children aged 14 years and above can be employed during school vacations. The Minister can restrict the labour of youth in certain positions and work places if he or she determines that those positions or work places may endanger the youth's physical or mental health or development.

The Youth Labour Law also lays down conditions and restrictions on the hours during which a minor is permitted to work – according to his or her educational commitments.

Israeli law also distinguishes between child labour and apprenticeships. The Apprenticeship Law, 1953 governs the employment of minors as apprentices.

Minors must be paid a certain percentage of the minimum wage, depending on the minor's age and the minor's status as an employee or apprentice.

10.9. Recordkeeping Requirements

The Wage Protection Law requires the employer to include comprehensive information in the pay slips to its employees. This information includes: details of the employee (name, ID no., term of employment, etc.), specific details as to the salary – scope of employment, calendar period covered by the pay slip, number of work days worked, number of hours worked, vacation days and sick days (due, accrued and taken), detailed information on salary paid – including payment for overtime and weekend/holiday work, recuperation/recreation payment (see further at Section 11 below), amounts subject to income tax and social security and amounts upon which pension and other social benefits are determined, deductions from salary – income tax, social security, health tax, provident funds and the total deductions for social benefits, method by which salary is paid and updated legal minimum wage per month and hour.

a. Information That Must Be Maintained

Employers are required to maintain a record of the information that is detailed on the employee's pay slips, including working time of each of their employees. This can be effected either by mechanical means, digitally or electronically or by compelling the employees to sign daily timesheets to be approved by the employer. While it is the employer's obligation to meet this provision, it requires the cooperation and participation of the employee.

During 2017, the National Labour Court considered the legitimacy of requiring employees to report their attendance using fingerprint and biometric attendance mechanisms. In its decision the Court addressed the right to privacy, and especially the right to privacy in the workplace. Issues on the right to privacy are dealt with further at Section 22.1 below. Specifically with regard to the biometric attendance clock the Court found that a person's fingerprint constitutes 'private information' and the use of such an attendance clock infringes the right to privacy. The case states the conditions for the legitimate use of a biometric attendance mechanism: (i) the employee gives informed consent – the case lists numerous details that the employer has to provide about the system for the consent to be informed; (ii) the consent is freely given and can be retracted and the employee is informed of such; (iii) the use of the system is reasonable, for a legitimate purpose which cannot be satisfied by less invasive measures. The Court pointed out that in its opinion there will usually be a less invasive measure that should be preferred.

b. Records That Must Be Retained

See subsection (a) above. In addition the employer is required to keep the following records:

(a) Under the Annual Vacation Law, 1951 – a vacation record detailing the name of the employee (first and family), his/her father's name, ID number, date of commencement of employment, period of vacation given, vacation pay paid and date of payment, date the employee failed to turn up for work, date of redemption of vacation pay and date of payment.

(b) Under the Hours of Work and Rest Law, 1951 – the name of the employee (first and family), his/her father's name, ID number, employee's address, date of commencement of employment with employer, hours of work, weekly hours of rest, overtime, payment for overtime, payment for work on weekly rest, termination of employment with employer.

c. Failure to Maintain Required Records

Failure to provide a salary slip containing all the details as required by law is a criminal offence subject to a fine (this can be doubled in severe cases).

Note also that civil and criminal liability may be imposed under the 2011 Law.

10.10. Reductions in Compensation Caused by Economic Downturn

There is no specific legislative provision addressing reductions in compensation caused by economic downturn. In practical terms, the employer can turn to employees and request the employees' consent to a deduction in the salary and/or benefits being provided to them where economics require the same, but subject to the minimum salary (and any other minimum protections afforded to employees). In such case, if the employee or employees agree – all well and good. If the employee does not agree, then the deduction in salary and/or benefits can be regarded as a worsening of the terms and conditions of employment, entitling the employee to resign and receive full severance pay under the Severance Pay Law, 1968.

As a matter of good practice, it makes sense for employers – when faced with the economic necessity of reducing salary and/or benefits to talk the employees through the process and explain the situation with a view to trying to reduce the possible negative impact on the work force. However, at the end of the day – whether the employer fires an employee who does not accept the reduction or whether such employee simply walks out of his or her own volition – such employee is entitled to the full severance package.

10.11. Checklist of Dos and Do Nots

(a) Make sure you pay wages that are not lower than the minimum wages in Israel.
(b) Do not make any deductions from wages or salaries without checking that they are permitted.
(c) Make sure that wages are paid on time.
(d) Make sure employees are not exceeding the amount of permitted over time, that over time is recorded and employees compensated in a way compliant with legal requirements.
(e) Check the age of employee candidates and only employ minors in accordance with the specific rules applicable to child labour.

11. OTHER WORKING CONDITIONS AND BENEFITS: BY STATUTE, COLLECTIVE AGREEMENTS OR COMPANY POLICY

Before dealing with the items listed below, mention should also be made of the employee's right to receive a recreation allowance (dmei havra'a) and transportation to work allowance (unless they have a vehicle supplied by the employer or they live in close proximity to the work place) under Israeli law. Additional benefits (e.g., contribution to telephone and vehicle expenses, stock options, additional salary, bonuses, further education fund, presents on High Holidays, etc.) may be due under individual or collective work agreements or are sometimes customary.

11.1. Health and Other Insurance

Pursuant to the National Health Insurance Law 1994, every person recognized as an Israeli resident is entitled to certain health services.

While there are certain exemptions, the National Health Insurance payments are mandatory and are paid directly to the National Health Institute. The amount of the payment is determined by salary or income level and is withheld from the employee's salary or wages. The employee is entitled to receive medical treatment, hospitalization and drugs from the sick funds.

Note also in addition to the list of leaves of absence below that, under Israeli law, the employer must pay the employee who was on reserve duty in the army his regular salary. The employer is entitled to reimbursement from the National Insurance Institute for these payments. Compulsory army reserve duty days are not included in the calculation of annual leave.

11.2. Pension and Retirement Benefits

The pension scheme in Israel is covered by national insurance and also a mandatory pension insurance requirement (and any private pension plans which are arranged by employers or individuals). The national insurance law supplies minimal benefits.

The General Collective Agreement (Framework) for Comprehensive Pension Insurance in Israel was extended by an Extension Order and is now applicable to all the employers and employees in Israel (men – from age 21, women – from age 20), unless they are subject to a pension arrangement that is more favourable to the employee.

Under the Collective Agreement (as extended), each of the employer and the employee is obliged to disburse to a pension fund or insurance policy a certain percentage of the Insured Income (being the lower of the employee's salary or the average salary in Israel). These disbursements are on account of the employee's pension. In addition, the employer is obliged to disburse to a pension fund or insurance policy on account of the employee's severance pay a further certain percentage (see also section 5.2 above on the General Collective Agreement (Framework)).

During 2015 and 2016, major changes have been introduced to the Israeli pension markets through amendments to the Control of Financial Services (Pension Counselling, Marketing and Pension Clearing System) Law, 5765-2005 ('Pension Advice Law') and also to the Control of Financial Services (Provident Funds) Law, 5765-2005 ('Pension Funds Law'). In essence, greater choice has now been afforded to the employee in seeking consultation about, and selecting, a pension product and the legislature has sought to break down the linkages between the amount of the disbursement on account of pension and the pension product itself. Thus the employer can no longer condition the rate of disbursement on the identity of the pension product. In addition, where an employee has not selected a pension fund, there are two default funds which are to be used – Meitav Dash Provident & Pension Ltd and Halman Aldubi Provident and Pension Funds Ltd.

With regard to the rate of disbursement, under the Collective Agreement (as Extended), each of the employer and the employee is obliged to disburse certain amounts to a pension fund or an insurance policy. The rates were finalized during 2016 and are now employee contribution of 6% and employer contribution of 6.5%. The employer's contribution includes disability insurance and may rise up to 7.5% if required in order to cover at least 75% of the employee's salary. Employers (and indeed employees) should seek legal advice when preparing employment agreements to ensure that these provisions are in line with the law as it has been changed.

Certain sectors may be subject to other rules. For instance, industry employees are subject to the Industrial Sector Extension Order – Framework for Comprehensive Pension Insurance in Industry, 2006.

In some sectors it is common practice for the contributions to pension funds or management insurance plans to exceed the statutory minimum.

There is also a law from 2014 to regulate the division of pension savings as between couples which have separated.

11.3. Vacation and Holiday Payments on Termination

The entitlement to vacation is covered by the Annual Leave Law, 1951. The Law – as with many of the employment laws containing minimum rights – is a cogent law, which sets forth the minimum rights of the employee with respect to vacation, and out of which the parties cannot contract. The minimum number of paid vacation days to which an employee is entitled under this law increases with seniority and ranges between fourteen and twenty-eight days (including the days of the weekend). For employees working a five-day week, the law has been amended so that the minimum is for the first four years of employment is equal to the minimum for the fifth year of employment and is twelve work days (sixteen days including the weekend). As with all the minimum rights provided under Israeli law, the parties are free to agree to greater rights.

Under this law, the vacation should be taken during the last month of the year or the next year. With the employer's consent, at least seven days' should be taken and the balance of accrued but unused vacation can be carried only over an additional two years – not for payment at that time, but for future use.

The right to payment in lieu of paid vacation leave arises only at the time of termination of the employment agreement. It is prohibited by law (with criminal sanctions) to make payment in lieu of vacation during the term of the employment agreement. Although it should be noted that, if the employment agreement provides for vacation entitlement in excess of the minimum provided by the Law, the employee and employer can also agree that the employee will be paid in lieu with respect to such excess during the period of employment.

11.4. Leaves of Absence

a. Personal Leave

Leave for personal reasons (save for those specifically addressed in this Section 11.4 below) forms part of the annual vacation entitlement and the minimum entitlements covered by the Annual Leave Law (see Section 11.3 above).

b. Medical or Sick Leave

Under the Sick Pay Law 1976, the entitlement to paid sick leave accumulates at a rate of one and one half days per month of employment, up to a maximum of ninety days. An employee can use this entitlement to take paid sick leave if such employee's parent, spouse or child is ill – the exact number of days depends on the circumstances (whether parent, spouse or child and whether the employee is a single parent, the nature of the sickness, etc.).

The Sick Pay Law provides that the sick pay to be actually paid will now be at a rate of 50% of the salary in respect of the second and third days of sick leave and, as from the fourth day, the employee will be entitled to sick pay at the rate of 100%. Under the provisions of the law sick pay does not have to be paid for the first day of illness, although some employers pay 100% of the salary for the whole period, including the first day. The law also addresses employees who work on a less than full month basis.

The general rule is that the sick pay entitlement that accumulated during the period of employment cannot be redeemed in money at the end of the employment, although in some collective agreements certain rights to redeem unused sick days can be found.

c. Bereavement Leave

An employee is entitled to paid time off during the seven days' mourning period following the death of a first-degree relative.

d. Family Leave

Family leave (save for those specifically addressed in this Section 11.4) forms part of the annual vacation entitlement and the minimum entitlements covered by the Annual Leave Law (see Section 11.3 above).

e. Pregnancy Leave

Statutory leave for pregnancy is part of the maternity leave. Up to seven weeks of the maternity leave may be taken before delivery.

Leave may be taken before delivery where determined by a medical practitioner as being in the interests of the employee's health or that of the unborn child. In the latter case, the leave required up to thirty days is on account of sick leave, such leave in excess of thirty days is subject to special support from the National Insurance.

An employee who has undergone a miscarriage may be absent from work for a period of one week after the miscarriage. A physician may extend the required absence period until up to six weeks.

An employee who is undergoing in vitro fertilization procedures or fertility treatment is entitled to paid sick leave with respect to the period required for the procedure or treatment and as certified by a physician.

f. Maternity Leave

The Employment of Women Law, 1954 regulates pregnancy and maternity leave. It is possible to take up to twenty-six weeks' maternity leave (the employee may take less than twenty-six weeks) of which – currently – fifteen weeks will be paid maternity leave. The salary is paid by the National Insurance and the employer pays the employee's social benefits during this period. As noted above, in absence of medical reasons, a maximum of seven weeks can be taken prior to delivery.

The entitlement to maternity leave is now also extended to a spouse whose partner works independently.

As a general rule, the mother and father can share part of the maternity/paternity leave. Note that, in addition, the father's right to be absent after the birth of a child has been increased to five days (first three on account of accumulated vacation days and the remainder on account of accumulated sick leave). In addition the father is entitled to seven days' maternity leave during the same period as the mother's maternity leave on account of the mother's paid maternity leave and where the mother has given a written waiver of her right during that period. The father also has certain rights where for example the mother is hospitalized.

g. Injury at Work

There is no specific provision in Israeli law regulating leave of absence for purposes of injuries sustained while at or going to and from the work place.

Employees who are injured at work or while travelling to or from work are entitled to receive compensation from the National Insurance – see also below at Section 12.

11.5. Checklist of Dos and Do Nots

(a) Pay mandatory allowances, such as recreation allowance and transportation to work allowance.
(b) Make sure that each of employer and employee contributes at least the minimal amounts as mandated by the General Collective Agreement (Framework) for Comprehensive Pension Insurance in Israel and the Extension Order that expanded it.
(c) Consider carefully how to deal with severance pay obligations that exceed the employers' disbursements on account of severance pay made under the General Collective Agreement (Framework) for Comprehensive Pension Insurance in Israel and the Extension Order that expanded it.
(d) Make sure that employees are entitled to at least the minimum number of vacation days prescribed by law and that they take the minimum number of vacation days as prescribed by law.
(e) Do not terminate the employment of a sick or injured employee before he or she were able to fully use their accrued sick day allowance.

12. WORKERS' COMPENSATION

12.1. Overview

The National Insurance is the Israeli equivalent of social security. It is regulated by the National Insurance Law, 1968. The employee and employer both have to contribute to the National Insurance payments. National Insurance provides not only for disability compensation in case of work accidents or occupational diseases, but also for unemployment benefits, old-age benefits, maternity allowance and other benefits.

Employees who are injured at work or while travelling to or from work are entitled to receive compensation. Initial compensation can be claimed from the National Insurance Institute.

It should also be noted that the regular pension schemes as well as those under the General Collective Agreement (Framework) for Comprehensive Pension Insurance in Israel contain an element for loss of earning capacity.

In addition, the employee may file a lawsuit against the employer to recover further compensation. The calculation of compensation to be paid by the employer will take into account any amounts recovered by the employee from the National Insurance Institute.

12.2. Checklist of Dos and Do Nots

(a) Do make sure all contributions required to be paid under the National Insurance Law are paid in full.
(b) Double check all pension scheme payment requirements.

13. COMPANY'S OBLIGATIONS TO PROVIDE SAFE AND HEALTHY WORKPLACE

13.1. Overview of Safety and Environmental Laws and Regulations

While there are numerous and detailed safety precaution measures applicable to employers, the Occupational Safety Ordinance [New Version] 1970 (the 'Ordinance') and the regulations promulgated pursuant thereto provide the main source of work place safety standards.

Under the Labour Inspection (Organization) Law 1954, a supervisory system for the implementation of the Occupational Safety Ordinance and regulations promulgated pursuant thereto was introduced. This is the Israel Institute for Occupational Safety and Hygiene (IIOSH), which is Israel's national public institution concerned with the workplace safety and health. In accordance with the law, the main objective of IIOSH is to promote safety and hygiene at the workplace, via:

(a) safety training and promotion;
(b) assistance in selecting safety representatives, organizing safety committees and guiding their activities;
(c) assisting the Labour Inspectorate in its activity;
(d) advising the Minister of Labour and Welfare on the matters concerning occupational safety and hygiene.

It should be noted that some fields of the work force may have specific rules and regulations on health and safety.

13.2. Requirements

The detailed requirements under the Ordinance and the Regulations promulgated pursuant thereto are numerous. However, in general terms, under the Ordinance the employer is required to do the following:

(a) prepare a safety management plan – this is a requirement which entered into force in August 2014 and the employer is required to establish a consistent pro-active safety management plan for the workplace. The plan should include – *inter alia* – sections as follows: A description of the workplace; the occupational health and safety policy of the workplace (including aims, measures, standards, guidelines and levels of risk); a description of the occupational health and safety system at the workplace and the set of treatments and responses to safety events and emergencies; risk management – assessing risks, identifying sources of risk, evaluation of risks, assessing means and determining guidelines and checks of risks; an employment safety training plan; a plan for testing and monitoring occupational and environmental safety testing equipment and materials; a plan for performing occupational medical tests. A person at management level is to be appointed in charge of health and safety at work and for the approval of the plan. The employer should allocate time and resources for implementing the plan;
(b) ensure a clean environment free from effluvia and dry;
(c) ensure that the working place will not be so overcrowded as to cause risk of injury to the health of employees;
(d) ensure effective and suitable ventilation, lighting and temperature;
(e) ensure safety of employees (fencing of machinery; access and passage; surfaces, stairs & ladders; lifts; chains, ropes & lifting tackle, dangerous fumes; explosive or inflammable dust, fumes or substances; steam boilers, receivers & containers; air receivers);
(f) ensure safety provisions are in place in case of fire;
(g) ensure adequate supply of wholesome drinking water;
(h) ensure adequate rest rooms, seating arrangements, and so on.

13.3. Rights of Employees

It is fair to conclude that employees are entitled to work in a safe and healthy work place. Employees are also entitled to be able to report incidents without the risk of being victimized. Where the nature of the work and work place require, employees should also be provided with necessary training, protective equipment, instruction manuals and other information.

13.4. Rights of Employer

The Ordinance does not itself grant rights to employers. Rather the purpose of the Ordinance (and the Regulations promulgated pursuant thereto) is to place obligations on employers to provide a healthy and safe working environment to employees. The employer does have certain rights regarding proceedings (rights to defend itself and rights to have proceedings continued against the actual offender) for example, where it is the employee himself or herself, which has violated the applicable provision and the employer has used due diligence to enforce such provision).

13.5. Specific Standards

By powers vested under the Ordinance, the Israeli Minister of Industry Trade and Labour may promulgate specific regulations regarding the safety and health of the work place.

In 1999, the Israeli Standard on Safety and Health Management – IS 18000 – was issued and is an adoption of the OHSAS 18001. Complementing guidelines for this standard were the British Standard 8800 and the Australian/New Zealand Standard 4804.

13.6. Injury or Accident at Work

Under the Accidents and Occupational Diseases (Notification) Ordinance 1945, detailed written notice must be sent of accidents arising out of and in the course of employment of any worker and causing loss of life or disablement of such worker for more than three days as well as of occupational diseases. Notice is to be sent to the occupational safety inspectorate appointed by the Minister of Industry, Trade and Labour.

13.7. Workplace Violence

Note that section 202 of the Occupational Safety Ordinance [New Version] 1970 expressly provides that no employed person shall wilfully and without reasonable cause do anything likely to endanger him or her or another. This provision could, arguably, be used in aid of a situation of workplace violence. Aside from that provision which, it has to be said, does not directly address workplace violence, there are no specific statutory provisions which deal with violence in the workplace. However, and based on the said section 202, it would be fair to say that part of the employee's right to work in a safe and healthy environment would include the right to work in a violent-free work place. As noted above, in the paragraphs dealing with termination for disciplinary reasons and warnings and suspensions, the employer has tools at hand for dealing with violence on the part of the employee.

All sections of the Criminal Code prohibiting various types of violence apply in all respect to violence in the workplace.

13.8. Fines and Penalties

Violation of the Occupational Safety Ordinance [New Version] 1970 is a criminal offence. There are certain listed violations under this Ordinance, which carry specific fines, but in all other cases violations may be punishable with imprisonment or a fine.

It should be noted that, in case of employers, which are legal entities (companies, partnerships, etc.), personal liability will attach to directors, officers or partners unless he or she can provide that the violation was committed without his or her knowledge and he or she took reasonable steps to prevent its commission.

13.9. Checklists of Dos and Do Nots

(a) Ensure the compliance with all general safety standards and check existence of specific safety requirements with an expert in the relevant field of occupation.
(b) Make sure that employees receive necessary training, protective equipment, instruction manuals and other information.
(c) If an occupational disease or an accident occurs causing loss of life or disablement of workers for more than three days, provide detailed notice to the occupational safety inspectorate appointed by the Minister of Industry, Trade and Labour.

14. IMMIGRATION, SECONDMENT AND FOREIGN ASSIGNMENT

14.1. Overview Laws Controlling Immigration

It should be noted that Israel is, currently at the time of writing, a destination for migrant workers from Asia, Eastern Europe and Africa.

Under section 1 of the Entry into Israel Law, 1952, a person who is not an Israeli citizen may enter Israel by visa. A visitor's visa – B-2 Visa (tourist)

– is valid for up to three months from the date of arrival in Israel. Visitors who wish to enter Israel to work will require a special work visa – a B-1 Entry and Residence Visa (and the accompanying employment permit). A B-1 visa is required for any type of migrant worker wishing to enter Israel – whether a labourer (agricultural or otherwise), university lecturer, R&D scientist, technician, and so on.

Israel does not have immigration quotas as such. Having said that, the Israeli government does set annual quotas for the number of foreign workers permitted to enter and work in Israel with respect to certain sectors of the employment market (e.g., agriculture, construction) where the need for these foreign workers has been recognized. Individuals having Jewish origins are entitled to immigrate to Israel under the Law of Return 1950.

Over the years, and especially as a result of the rapid growth of the high-tech/bio-tech industry in Israel, this has resulted in different procedures being made available for those individuals wishing to enter Israel to work who fall within the definition of 'foreign expert'. It should be noted, in this respect, that Israel is a member of the World Trade Organization (WTO) and the General Agreement on Trade and Services (GATT). As such, Israel is committed to allow managers and executives of foreign multinational corporations to enter Israel in order to participate in foreign-invested projects in Israel. In addition, Israel is a party to bilateral agreements with various countries, which include a mutual commitment to facilitate employee relocation from one country to another.

The different procedures available are as follows:

(i) Foreign experts who engage in professions requiring higher academic education - B-1 work visa once granted will generally be up to one year from the date of approval. It can be extended and the maximum aggregate stay is five years or so. Since this is a single entry visa, the application should require multiple entry allowance.

(ii) Foreign experts who engage in trades requiring expertise but not requiring academic expertise - B-1 work visa once granted will generally be up to one year from the date of approval. It can be extended and the maximum aggregate stay is five years or so. Since this is a single entry visa, the application should require multiple entry allowance.

(iii) Foreign experts – working in Israel for up to three months with no extension. This is single entry only and a return visa '(inter-visa') should be applied for if the expert will need to leave and re-enter Israel.

(iv) Foreign expert – working in Israel for up to forty-five days with no extension. Applicable to nationals who are exempt from a tourist visa (for example from EU, USA, Japan, Austrialia, etc).

In addition, new trial visa procedures have been introduced:

(i) Innovation Visa – this procedure was introduced for foreign entrepreneurs – the trial is to extend over three years with approved entrepreneurs being able to stay in Israel for twenty four months. This is to allow foreign entrepreneurs to enter and work in Israel for the purpose of the development and establishment of technological ventures in Israel. The foreign entrepreneur will be hosted by one of twelve approved support frameworks. The foreign entrepreneur (not an Israel resident or citizen) will need to provide a declaration of sources of funds for their living expenses while in Israel and a specification of the support framework they intend to join and the acceptance of them by such support framework. The process is commenced with the Israeli Innovation Authority which will then decide whether to recommend the approval of visa to the Ministry of the Interior; and

(ii) Foreign experts in hi-tech and cyber companies – applicable to companies recognized by the Innovation Authority in Israel as technological knowledge-intensive companies.

For situations not falling within any of the above 'foreign expert' or 'innovation visa' categories, it should be noted, by way of general background, that – neither the Law nor any of the Regulations which have been promulgated – refers specifically to the term 'business visitor'. The official approach taken is that individuals entering Israel for a short term for business purposes, such as to conduct negotiations or to review investment opportunities can enter under a visitor's visa. Entering Israel to perform productive work requires a work visa. In this respect, the term 'work' is also not defined in the Law (and nor is it defined in the Foreign Workers' Law). This can make the determination of whether a given individual falls within one category or the other difficult. Nevertheless, it is fair to say that – notwithstanding the absence of definition – the Israeli official approach is that 'work' is any productive activity performed in Israel which presents an economic value. Typically, the criteria, which will be taken into account in determining whether a visitor is seeking to enter Israel in order to 'work', will include:

(a) the purpose and nature of the visit to Israel;
(b) the length of the visit;
(c) the location of payment of the salary;
(d) the nature of the business relationship.

Of these factors, the major criterion, which will be taken into account, is the first one – the purpose and nature of the visit to Israel. The length of the visit is not conclusive in the sense that a shorter stay does not necessarily mean the individual is not entering for the purpose to 'work'. For instance, conducting training and installing, repairing and maintaining equipment are considered to be work and require a work visa, even though the duration of the stay is not long. For such visits a special work visa for forty-five days can be applied for. Nevertheless, it is perhaps true to say that the longer the stay, the more readily it might be inferred that the visitor is staying in Israel for the purpose of working.

Other factors, which can be taken into account include whether the visitor brings his or her family to Israel, how the visitor travels in Israel (rented car or own vehicle, for example), where the visitor will be residing while in Israel (own accommodation or hotel). The location of the payment of the salary may be indicative but the fact that the visitor is paid by a foreign employer is not conclusive in determining such visitor as a business visitor.

On a slightly different note regarding immigration, in 2006 the Anti Trafficking Law, 2006 entered into force. This law is intended to cover a broad crime of trafficking for various purposes: prostitution, sexual crimes, slavery or forced labour, removal of organs, pornography and using the body of a person to give birth to a baby who is then removed from the parent. The penalty for violation of the law is up to sixteen years imprisonment (increased to twenty years if the victim was a minor) depending on the violation. This law is designed to combat trafficking in persons and also places emphasis on the prohibition of slavery and forced labour. Through this law, new offences have been introduced to the Penal Code, 1977 (e.g., trafficking in human beings for the purpose of slavery or forced labour; holding a person under conditions of slavery; forced labour; exploitation of vulnerable populations; abduction for the purpose of slavery or forced labour and conveying a person beyond the boundaries of a State and causing a person to leave a State for the purposes of prostitution or slavery). These criminal offences are alongside the regulatory measures designed to protect foreign workers (see Section 14.4 below).

14.2. Recruiting, Screening and Hiring Process

The recruitment, screening and hiring process to be followed will depend on the type of entry and work permit being applied for. The necessity for obtaining an entry and work permit should be made clear to all applicants.

Note that, with respect to Israeli recruitment agencies, the permitted recruitment fees are capped pursuant to the Employment Service (Recruitment Fees) Regulations, 2006. In addition, the Employment Service (Provision of Information) Regulations, 2006 require the recruitment agency to provide foreign workers with all relevant information regarding the permitted recruitment fees and other worker rights.

14.3. Obligation of Employer to Enforce Immigration Laws

Employers may be prosecuted for violations of Israeli labour laws, including the Foreign Workers Law, 1991. It should be noted that, this law – as amended in 2001 – was to ensure that foreign workers receive employee protection rights.

14.4. Fines and Penalties

Under the Foreign Workers Law, 1991, the employer can be fined for violating the provisions of that law. There have been instances where – on appeal from a first instance decision by the State – the appellate court has increased the initial fine imposed on the employer.

Pursuant to the Employment Service Law (Amendment No. 14), 2004 it is a criminal offence for an employer to collect illegal excessive recruitment fees from foreign workers. This is a crime which is punishable by up to six months imprisonment and/or a fine of up to NIS 200,000.

14.5. Secondment/Foreign Assignment

Generally, Israeli labour laws do not apply to Israelis working overseas. Israeli law would not prohibit the parties from agreeing contractually to regulate their relationship with respect to employment outside Israel (which would not in itself be subject to Israeli law) as if Israeli law applies (although this could contradict the laws in the actual place of employment).

In addition, where the employee is sent temporarily on secondment to work outside Israel but for an Israeli employer, Israeli law may be found to govern the employment relationship even in absence of an express provision regarding the same.

The Israeli labour laws, which provide for the minimum rights and entitlements of employees, apply to all employees within Israel and would apply also to foreign nationals working in Israel (with or without a visa).

14.6. Checklist of Dos and Do Nots

(a) Where the individual is seeking to enter Israel to work, it is recommended to commence with the appropriate procedure to obtain a work permit a sufficient period of time and at least several months in advance.

(b) Make sure that there is no violation of Israeli labour laws also with respect to foreign workers.

15. RESTRICTIVE COVENANTS AND PROTECTION OF TRADE SECRETS AND CONFIDENTIAL INFORMATION

15.1. Overview

In cases where employment agreements are reduced to writing, it is common to find specific provisions addressing ownership of intellectual property developed by the employee within the employment, use and maintain in secrecy of confidential information of the employer, restrictive covenants and non-solicitation provisions.

15.2. The Law of Trade Secrets

Under the Commercial Torts Law 1999, there is a general prohibition on using the trade secrets of others. The prohibition is applicable to employees, whether a specific prohibition is included in the employment agreement or not. In certain industries and also with certain seniority of employees, it is customary to include more specific provisions addressing the prohibition against the use of trade secrets of the employer – these provisions are generally enforceable.

15.3. Restrictive Covenants and Non-compete Agreements

As a general rule, Israeli law permits reasonable non-competition clauses that actually protect the interests of the employer and the employee, both during the term of employment and thereafter. Such restriction has to be reasonable with respect to the time period and geographical limitations it imposes. However, after the term of employment the courts will not enforce non-compete clauses where there is no 'legitimate interest' of the former employer. The courts narrowly interpret such 'legitimate interest' such as real damage to the employer's trade secrets (such as customer lists or unique marketing strategies, etc.), cases of specific consideration provided solely for the non-compete undertaking, and actions which are in violation of the duty to act in good faith on behalf of the employee. Even where the employer can show that the employee possesses the employer's trade secrets, the employer will be required to prove that there is a reasonable chance that the employee will use them. Note that the Israeli courts have held that the employee's own professional experience and abilities belong to the employee and that there can be no prohibition against their use.

15.4. Checklist of Dos and Do Nots

(a) Before entering into an employment relationship, check if employee is subject to any non-compete or similar obligations that could be violated. If there are, evaluate the legal risks.
(b) Do not assume that non-compete provisions in the employment agreements will be enforced. The enforceability of such provisions has to be checked carefully on a case-by-case basis.

16. PROTECTION OF WHISTLEBLOWING CLAIMS

16.1. Overview

This is covered by the Protection of Employees (Exposure of Offences of Unethical Conduct and Improper Administration) Law, 1997. By terms of this law, an employer must not impair an employee's terms of engagement and must not dismiss an employee who has submitted a complaint against his or her employer or against any other employee of that employer or who assisted in submitting such a complaint.

The Regional Labour Court has sole jurisdiction over proceedings for violation of this law. The court may award compensation if it deems fit –even if no monetary loss was caused and may also issue an injunction or mandatory order (including one to revoke the dismissal). Note though that the power to issue injunctions or mandatory orders is limited to cases where the employer is a public body (as listed in the Schedule to this law) or to employers who employ more than twenty-five employees.

If the court finds that the complaint was false, and was made in circumstances that the complainant knew or ought to have known it to be false, then the court shall not grant relief under the law. In addition, if the court also finds the complaint was not made in good faith, the complainant may be ordered to pay compensation to the employer or to the employee against whom the complaint was made.

Relief will only be granted under the law in respect of a complaint to which all of the following apply:

(a) the complaint was brought in good faith;
(b) the complaint was submitted in respect of the commission of an offence under any enactment in the workplace or in connection with

the breach of legislation at the workplace or a breach of any legislation relating to the employee's work or the employer's field of business activity or in a public body – also where the complaint was filed with respect to unethical conduct or improper administration;

(c) the complaint was filed with an authority competent to receive complaints or competent to investigate the matter subject of the complaint.

There is a special prescription period of twelve months which applies to the relief available under this law (i.e., the court will not hear a claim in respect of a complaint which was filed more than twelve months after the date on which the grounds for complaint arose).

For those who are employed in public service, the provisions of the Encouragement of Ethical Conduct in the Public Service Law, 1992 also apply. Under this law, in cases of a justified complaint by a public servant of a corrupt act or other infringement of ethical conduct, the State President or the Speaker of the Knesset (after consultation with the State President) may award a certificate of merit to the complainant.

16.2. Checklist of Dos and Do Nots

- Do not impair an employee's terms of engagement or dismiss an employee who has submitted a complaint against the employer or against any other employee of that employer or who assisted in submitting such a complaint.

17. PROHIBITION OF DISCRIMINATION IN THE WORKPLACE

17.1. Overview of Anti-discrimination Laws

Israel's Declaration of Independence proclaimed equality as one of the underlying principles of the new State. The enforcement of equality at the workplace began in the early 1950s with prohibition against the discharge of pregnant workers. This principle was given a major push during the 1970s, when the National Labour Court handed down a judgment, which invalidated one of the sections of a collective agreement, which discriminated against female flight attendants. Comprehensive legislation followed – the Employment Equal Opportunities Law, 1988 (which replaced the Employment Equal Opportunities Law, 1981) prohibits discrimination as aforesaid. This legislation prohibits discrimination on the basis of race, religion, sex, personal status, marital status, nationality or country of origin, sexual orientation, age, disability, political affiliation or army reserve service. The law also provides that setting conditions that are not relevant is discriminatory, the law further provides that the burden to prove that there was no discrimination will lie with the employer if the employer demanded information with respect to one of the protected statuses.

In 2008 the Equal Opportunities Commission was set up (further to an amendment to the Employment Equal Opportunities Law). This Commission has a wide range of duties including fostering public awareness by means of education, training and public relations; promoting programmes and activities; cooperating with other entities including employees and employers; conducting research; intervening – with the leave of the court – in legal proceedings; handling complaints concerning violation of the law – such as filing civil actions in the courts; applying to the courts for general orders to instruct employers to take general measures.

Under the law, discrimination against employees or prospective employees is prohibited during all stages of the employment process: hiring; terms and conditions of employment; promotion; training; dismissal and severance pay; and retirement benefits. The Regional and National Labour courts have ruled that the concept of 'freedom of contract' does not justify discrimination (e.g., such as that evidenced by paying different salaries to men and women for the same work done).

In addition, and as noted further in each of the appropriate subsections of this Section 17 below, there are various specific items of legislation, which apply to issues of non-discrimination.

Reference should also be made to the Basic Law: Human Dignity and Liberty. This Basic Law is intended: 'to defend Human dignity and liberty in order to establish in a Basic Law the values of the State of Israel as a Jewish and democratic state'. Of course, reference should also be made to the general obligation to act in good faith and in the customary manner.

The Labour Courts are empowered to award damages without proof of actual economic damage. They may also issue orders to reinstate an employee discharged in violation of this law. These remedies are unusual in Israeli law – the common remedy would be compensation upon proof of damage (and it is also available in these situations). The law transfers the burden of proof to the employer after the worker has proven prima facie discrimination.

Violation of the Employment Equal Opportunities Law may also constitute a criminal offence leading to the imposition of a fine.

17.2. Age Discrimination

This is covered by the Employment (Equal Opportunities) Law, 1988.

When determining whether there is discrimination on account of age, the court may (depending on the circumstances of the case) need to consider the relevant comparison group. For example, in one case, which concerned the age of retirement of civil servants as a whole (at the time, 65) by contrast with that of police officers or wardens employed for more than ten years (at the time, 55) (who are also civil servants), the court found that the relevant comparison group was that of civil servants as a whole. In another case, the court found that termination on grounds of age alone (on the facts, the court found there was no other reason for terminating the employment relationship nor was it consented to by the employee) when the female employee in question had reached 60 years, violated the Employment (Equal Opportunities) Law, 1988. The National Labour Court has also decided that employees reaching the mandatory age of retirement can approach employers with a request to continue working even after reaching this age. While the employer does not have to accept the request automatically, it is required to consider the same properly, in good faith and without prejudice, taking into account all relevant circumstances.

17.3. Race Discrimination

This is expressly prohibited by the Employment (Equal Opportunities) Law, 1988. See also Section 24 below on affirmative action.

17.4. Sex Discrimination/Sexual Harassment

The general prohibition against discrimination based on gender is found not only in the Employment (Equal Opportunities) Law, 1988 but also in the 'Basic Law' Human Liberty and Dignity.

The Women's Equal Right Law, 1951 provides that 'a man and a woman shall have equal status with regard to any legal proceeding; any provision of law which discriminates, with regard to any legal proceeding, against women as women, shall be of no effect'. This law was amended in 2000, and section 6 of the amended law provides that every woman and man have equal right to a dignified existence, which includes equal treatment in the areas of employment, education, health, housing and social welfare.

Originally, the Male and Female Workers Equal Pay Law, 1964 guaranteed equal pay to women and men workers for equal work. Few cases were brought under this law. In 1996, this law was replaced by another law of the same name. The 1996 law includes a definition of equivalent work and also enables the appointment of job evaluation experts and compels employers to give information and allow class actions. In 2004, the Retirement Age Law, 2004 was enacted to provide for more equable norms regarding retirement age. The mandatory retirement age for men is 67 while women can choose to retire between the ages of 62 and 67.

In one case, the Tel-Aviv Labour Court found discrimination by an employer against a male employee who the employer wished to have replaced by a female employee. In that case, the court determined that, in order to prove discrimination, the employee only needs to demonstrate that the prohibited discrimination was actually a factor for the employer's decision, even if it was not the only or main reason.

Regarding sexual harassment, this is primarily covered in the Prevention of Sexual Harassment Law, 1998. Section 3 of the Prevention of Sexual Harassment Law, 1998 lists those acts which constitute sexual harassment. Some require that the victim has expressed his or her lack of interest in order for the situation to constitute an act of sexual harassment, whereas others do not. One situation, which is of particular relevant to the workplace, namely where an individual exploits a position of authority does not require that the victim has expressed his or her lack of interest.

During 2014 this Law was amended to include in the definition of sexual harassment, the publication of a photograph, film or tape of a person or the editing or combination of photographs, films or tapes, done without consent, which focus on the sexuality of the subject, in circumstances which are likely to humiliate or degrade the subject. Certain defences are available to publisher: (i) whether the publication was made in good faith, taking into account the circumstances of the publication, its contents, forms, scope and aims; or (ii) whether the publication was made for a valid purpose; or (iii) whether the publication involves a matter of public interest which justifies it in the circumstances of the case, but only if the publication is not false and does not criticize or contain an opinion on a public officer in relation to his or her position and also provided that the publication does not derogate from being reasonable in order to achieve its goals.

The Israeli Supreme Court has adopted a rigorous approach regarding sexual harassment in the workplace. In this respect, the Supreme Court has determined that the phrase 'position of authority' is not limited only to the employer or immediate superior but also can include any person who holds a position of power, influence or authority. In addition, the Supreme Court has found that sexual harassment may exist in the manner in which the culprit addresses or talks to the victims (and is not limited to conduct).

The local labour courts have also interpreted the obligation of the employer to conduct investigations into sexual harassment allegations in a way which extends beyond the protection of the victim of the alleged harassment alone. The employer's obligation to carry out such an investigation is interpreted as an obligation intended to protect the entire workforce, including potential future victims and even those whose reputation may be been wrongly tainted by rumors. The possibility of completely avoiding an investigation should be limited to exceptional cases only (e.g: where a criminal investigation is underway and it is suspected that the investigation by the employer might thwart it or disrupt it, or where the perpetrator is no longer working with the employer and his or her version cannot be obtained).

Under the Prevention of Sexual Harassment Law, 1998, an employer is required to take such steps as are reasonable in the circumstances to prevent sexual harassment or adverse treatment in the labour relations sphere. The employer is also obliged to deal with cases of sexual harassment or adverse treatment. Moreover, an employer who employs more than twenty-five employees is required to prescribe and publish a code of practice detailing the principal provisions of the law concerning sexual harassment and adverse treatment in the workplace and also detailing the procedures prescribed by the employer for handing complaints with respect to the same, including the appointment of a supervisor. This supervisor is required to handle complaints and take steps to raise employees' awareness of the same. It would be good practice to include the amended definition from 2014 (as to what constitutes sexual harassment) in the code of practice. This code of practice has to be published among the employees.

Sexual harassment in the work place may be a criminal offence and may also be the basis of a civil suit against the both the employer and the individual responsible for the harassment.

17.5. Handicap and Disability Discrimination

The Equal Rights for Handicapped Persons Law, 1998 protects the dignity and liberty of physically or mentally handicapped individuals and is designed to ensure their equal and active participation in all areas of life, including work. This law has created a new system of obligations for the State of Israel towards its disabled citizens. See further at paragraph 3.1 above on the obligations imposed on the employer regarding the recruitment of persons with disabilities.

The law contains operative provisions concerning not only employment but also public transport services and it also establishes the Commission for Equal Rights of Persons with Disabilities. With specific regard to employment, the law prohibits discrimination on the basis of disability and obliges employers to make reasonable work accommodations and requires appropriate representation of persons with disabilities within the work force.

By Regulations promulgated pursuant to the law, employers are obliged to provide each disabled employee with an accessible designated parking space for his or her exclusive use (this applies to employers who have at least six employees and has provided designated parking spaces for at least three of them). Note also that Regulations provide for employers' to receive a refund from the Government on expenses made in adjusting the work place to the disability, work and daily needs of disabled employees.

As a result of certain decisions of the Labour courts, the Equal Rights of Persons with Disabilities Employed as Rehabilitated Persons (Temporary Provisions) Law, 2007 was enacted. Under this law, a person whose work capacity is less than 19% shall not be considered an employee but rather a rehabilitated person. Thus, the entire body of employment laws does not apply, and instead the 2007 law gives a rehabilitated person the right to remuneration for work and decent work conditions concerning matters such as leave, sick pay, hours of work and travel expenses. This 2007 law supplements specific Regulations addressing adjustments to the minimum wage for persons who are at various levels of diminished work capacity as the result of a disability.

It should also be noted that, in 2007, Israel signed the Convention on the Rights of Persons with Disabilities.

17.6. National Origin Discrimination

This is expressly prohibited by the Employment (Equal Opportunities) Law, 1988. See also Section 24 below, affirmative action.

17.7. Religious Discrimination

This is prohibited by the Employment (Equal Opportunities) Law, 1988. In addition, section 9(c) of the Hours of Work and Rest Law, 1951 is also relevant – an employer may not discriminate against an employee who objects to working on the day of rest for religious reasons.

17.8. Military Status Discrimination

Section 2(a) of the Employment (Equal Opportunities) Law, 1988 also provides that an employer shall not discriminate among his employees on grounds, *inter alia*, of duration of military service.

Section 2A of that law further provides that employers shall not ask applicants for employment or employees for their military profile or make use of it for any purpose set forth in sections 2(a) 1 through 6 of said law (i.e., acceptance for employment, terms of employment, advancement in employment, vocational training, dismissal or severance pay, benefits and payments to employees in connection with their retirement). This prohibition does not apply to the General Security Service and the Institute for Intelligence and Special Assignments.

17.9. Pregnancy Discrimination

Section 9 of the Employment of Women Law, 1954 prohibits the discharge of a pregnant employee or the reduction of her hours of work, where such employee has been with the employer for more than six months (and maybe even in cases of employment of less than six months). It should be noted though that this law also allows the Minister of Labour and Welfare to issue a permit to an employer to discharge a pregnant worker in cases where the discharge is unrelated to her pregnancy. Discharge in violation of this law is void and considered a criminal offence. Discrimination on the basis of pregnancy is still prohibited under the Employment (Equal Opportunities) Law, which applies to all pregnant employees, even if they are not protected against dismissal under the Employment of Women Law.

In addition, the employer cannot discharge the worker during maternity leave. During a period of sixty days after the employee's return to work dismissal requires a permit.

Note also the provisions of section 4(a) 1 of the Employment (Equal Opportunities) Law. Where in accordance with the terms of employment customary at her place of work a woman employee has an entitlement by virtue of being a parent, such entitlement shall also be accorded to a male employee at the same workplace if (i) his spouse is an employee and she has not been absent from her work by virtue of her said right or has not claimed the right to such entitlement, or (ii) if the child is in his sole custody.

17.10. Marital Status Discrimination

This is expressly prohibited by the Employment (Equal Opportunities) Law 1988. In addition, the Single Parent Family Law 1992, expressly provides that a single parent is entitled, *inter alia*, to preference for vocational training under conditions and rules established by the Minister of Labour and Social Affairs.

17.11. Sexual Orientation Discrimination

This is expressly prohibited by the Employment (Equal Opportunities) Law, 1988. In a leading authority, both the Supreme Court of Israel and the National Labour Court found that a certain collective agreement was discriminatory in that a benefit which was provided – pursuant to such collective agreement – to married couples and to couples living as 'common law' man and wife, was not given to a male couple living together and making a home together.

17.12. Retaliation

In 2000, the Collective Agreements Law was amended to prohibit discrimination on grounds of participation, or failure to participate, in union activity or union organizing efforts. See also Section 23 below on whistle blowing.

17.13. Constructive Discharge

Section 5 of the Employment (Equal opportunities Law), 1988 provides that an employer shall not, for the purpose of remedying discrimination prohibited by section 2(a)(2) (discrimination for purpose of terms of employment), detract from the rights, or worsen the position, of any other employee.

17.14. Checklist of Dos and Do Nots

(a) Ensure the work environment is free of discrimination.
(b) All acts and omissions within the employment relationships should be carried out in good faith and in the customary manner.
(c) Be careful to provide a work place free of sexual harassment. Provide notification of the code in the manner prescribed by the law.
(d) Employer is required to make reasonable work accommodations and requires appropriate representation of persons with disabilities.
(e) Employers shall not ask applicants or employees for their military profile or make use of it with respect to the employment relationship.
(f) Employer shall not, for the purpose of remedying discrimination with respect to terms of employment, detract from the rights, or worsen the position, of any other employee.

18. SMOKING IN THE WORKPLACE

18.1. Overview

The Israel Restrictions on Smoking (Public Places) Law, 1983 prohibits smoking in a place specified in the Schedule to that law. The said Schedule includes 'a workplace', which is defined as any place in a building in which people are employed and which is not a dwelling. Smoking is permitted in a room which has been expressly permitted by the person in charge – after consulting with the employees – provided that in the smoking area there are no non-smokers and the area has proper working ventilation facilities and smoking in such area does not cause a nuisance in other parts of the building.

The law also requires the affixation of signs indicating the prohibition of smoking. Contravention of the law gives rise to fine. Contravention of the law – the obligation to affix signs – can be attributed to directors, partners and senior employees unless such person can provide that it was committed without his/her knowledge and he/she took all reasonable measures to ensure compliance.

18.2. Checklist of Dos and Do Nots

(a) Provide smoking area only as prescribed by law.
(b) Affix signs indicating the prohibition of smoking in other areas of the work place.

19. USE OF DRUGS AND ALCOHOL IN THE WORKPLACE

19.1. Overview

The Israeli legal environment is essentially void of reference to the rights and obligations of both employees and employers with respect to the handling of employee workplace substance abuse. The general criminal offences that prohibit drug use apply to the work place. Taking certain actions while under the influence of drugs or alcohol are also considered as criminal actions and civil torts. The employer is entitled to take disciplinary measures against an employee that attends work under the influence of drugs or alcohol. However, the general approach of Israeli law is that it does not allow physical or invasive testing.

Of course the above may not hold true in specific work place environments (such as the military and public transport).

19.2. Checklist of Dos and Do Nots

(a) In specific work place environments make sure any applicable regulations are applied.
(b) If employer has actual knowledge of substance abuse, disciplinary action might be applicable but should be applied only in accordance with the law (see also sections 4, 5 and 6 above).

20. AIDS, HIV, SARS, BLOODBORNE PATHOGENS

20.1. Overview

As already noted, as a general rule, the employer is not entitled to force an employee to undergo medical tests which are conducted on behalf of the work place and if an employee refuses to undergo such checks, this would not generally constitute a ground for the employer to take disciplinary or other action against the employee.

Where an employer sets medical tests as criteria for acceptance to the work place or as part of the performance or other checks, these tests should be relevant to the role and position of the employee or potential employee in question.

20.2. Checklist of Dos and Do Nots

(1) Employer should only require medical tests that are relevant to the role and position of the employee as criteria for acceptance to the work place.

21. DRESS AND GROOMING REQUIREMENTS

21.1. Overview

There is no general legislation regulating dress and grooming requirements in the workplace. Having said that, there may be specific regulations governing dress and grooming requirements in specific industries (such as, for example, the food industry or legal industry – appearances before courts, and in other areas where safety issues arise, etc.).

Rather, the Israel labour courts have addressed this issue on various occasions. The courts have had to balance between the conflicting rights of the employee (freedom of expression, basic right of respect, and the like) and the right of the employer to require that employees will – by their dress – reflect the image the employer wishes its business to broadcast. On the whole, the courts have favoured the employer's right of uniform appearance over the employee's rights.

Where the employer applies a dress code in the work place, such employer would be advised to inform potential employees of the same, since it is possible that this dress code could bring about a change in such employee's usual dress code (where, for example, a female employee will be required to wear skirts/dresses to work and not trousers). Note also that, where the employee breaks the dress code, this may not found a basis for not paying severance pay.

21.2. Checklist of Dos and Do Nots

(1) If a dress code applies in the work place, employer should inform potential employees of the same.

22. PRIVACY, TECHNOLOGY AND TRANSFER OF PERSONAL DATA

22.1. Privacy Rights of Employees

The privacy laws in Israel are primarily governed by the Protection of Privacy Law, 1981 ('Privacy Law"). Section 1 of this Law provides that a person's privacy shall not be violated without such person's consent. Section 2 goes on to define what constitutes damage to privacy and includes (as relevant for present purposes) the following: (i) the breach of a duty of confidentiality determined under law regarding the private matters of a person; (ii) the use of information as to the private matters of a person or the transfer of the same to another, which was not for the purpose it was provided; (iii) the publication or transfer of something that was obtained by way of damaging privacy pursuant to, *inter alia*, (i) and (ii) above. Please note that the term 'use' is defined to include, discovery, transfer and sending.

The Protection of Privacy Law further provides, in section 23B, that the transfer of information from a public entity is forbidden unless such information has been published to many in accordance with legal authority or is available to many in accordance with legal authority or the person to whom the information relates has given his/her consent to its transfer. Public entities are defined to include the government Ministries and other governmental institutions. The Protection of Privacy Law provides in section 23C for exceptions when such information may be transferred.

Section 4 of the Protection of Privacy Law provides that the violation of the right to privacy is a civil wrong. Section 5 of the Protection of Privacy law further provides that the person causing certain damages of privacy shall be subject to prison sentence of five years. After having said that, a civil or criminal claim under the Protection of Privacy Law must be a claim with substance (see section 6 of the Protection of Privacy Law).

In general terms, the National Labour Court has recognized the employee's right to privacy at the workplace, notwithstanding the employer's legitimate right to protect its assets and business. The employer's right to collect, use and store data relating to an employee or candidate employee will be construed more strictly and narrowly with respect to personal data than in other contexts where the employment relationship does not exist.

By virtue of the Privacy Law, an owner of a digital database is required to register such digital database where one of the following applies:

(a) the information is about more than 10,000 persons;
(b) the database includes sensitive information or personal data (e.g., information on a person's personality, private family relations, state of health, economic condition, vocational qualification, opinion and faith);
(c) the database includes information about persons and such persons, or others acting on their behalf, did not provide the information or did not consent to the provision thereof;
(d) the database belongs to a public body;
(e) the database is used for direct mail;
(f) The individuals whose information is on the database are provided with rights of perusal and correction.

The use of all information obtained must be lawful. For example, the information cannot be used to discriminate between employees or potential employees on a basis that is prohibited under Israeli law. Making incorrect information available to third parties may raise issues as to, *inter alia*, defamation.

Regulations, which entered into force in May 2018 (the Privacy Protection (Data Security) Regulations, 2017 are designed to provide universal standards for the protection of information and for the protection of personal data held in digital databases by various entities and bodies.

Pursuant to the Privacy Law, the Privacy Protection Authority ('PPA') was established as the body responsible for personal digital information and for the protection of all personal information held in digital databases. The head of the PPA is the Israeli Database Registrar. From time to time, the Database Registrar issues guidelines to clarify the manner in which the the PPA interprets the Privacy Law when exercising its enforcement powers.

For example, during 2017, guidelines published by the Database Registrar, address the right to view information which is stored digitally. The right to view is traditionally provided by means of the receipt of a 'printout' or 'presentation' given by the party holding the information. However, these means are not appropriate for current technological developments and digital collection and storage. In light of this, the Database Registrar has emphasized in these guidelines that information which is received and/or stored digitally (including correspondence, voice recordings, telephone conversations and films and videos) forms part of the database and, as such, all the provisions of the Privacy Law (including the obligation to register a database, to the extent required), including the right to view. It is within the scope of the authority of the Database Registrar to impose administrative fines for violations of the right to view.

In October 2017, the Database Registrar also published guidelines on the use of surveillance cameras at the workplace and within the employment relationship. The PPA recognizes that the employee has a right to privacy also at the workplace. The guidelines provide that such cameras should be used proportionately and in a manner which respects the employee's privacy (so of course cameras cannot be used in the bathrooms or changing rooms or, for example, in areas not freely available to the public). Cameras are to be used for a legitimate purpose (such as for employee safety, disciplinary supervision, assuring quality of business service or protecting employer's property). The employer should prepare a clear and detailed policy regarding the manner, scope and purposes of the use of the cameras in the workplace and employees should be informed of such policy. Exaggerated use of cameras in a manner that disproportionately prejudices an employee will expose the employer to administrative, civil and criminal sanctions. In some circumstances, this may also give rise to the employee's right to resign with full severance pay rights. It must be remembered that an employer is prohibited from photographing an employee without the latter's knowledge.

Guidelines have also been published addressing the use of outsourcing services for personal data processing and also addressing privacy protection during recruitment procedures and privacy protection by recruitment agencies.

The transfer of information abroad is permitted, subject to the provisions of the Protection of Privacy (Transfer of Information to Databases Outside the Borders of Israel) Regulations, 2001. In summary, these Regulations include the following requirements: (i) the laws of the State to which the information is to be transferred should guarantee a level of protection of the information no less than that provided in Israel (e.g., the manner in which information is collected and processed should be legal and just); and (ii) the information is to be held, used and provided solely for the same purpose as it was received; the stored information should be updated and accurate; and

(iii) an individual has the right to view information pertaining to him/herself. The Regulations also provide that – notwithstanding the requirements mentioned above – information can be transferred abroad if: (i) the individual has consent to such transfer; or (ii) the information is transferred to a corporation under the Control of the owner of the database from which the information is transferred, and the transferee has assured the protection of privacy post-transfer. Control means the ability to direct the corporation's acts (unless such ability derives solely from acting as an officer or director of the corporation). The possession of 50% or more of the means of control in a corporation raises a presumption of Control. The assurance of the transferee will require the transferee to undertake to effect the terms and conditions that apply to storing and using information in a database in Israel; or (iii) the information is transferred to a party to the European Treaty of Protection of the Individual's Rights in connection with Automatic Process of Sensitive Data and receives information from Member States of the European Community – or is transferred to a State which has been recognized by the Registrar of Databases as one that has an authority dedicated to protect privacy and with which State an agreement to cooperate with such authority has entered into effect.

In the event that the information is transferred abroad in accordance with the above-mentioned rules, the owner of the database must assure, by a written undertaking of the transferee that such transferee is taking sufficient measures to protect the privacy of the persons to whom the information refers, and guarantees that the information will not be transferred to any other person, either in the same State or in any other State.

Personal data which has been made entirely anonymous is no longer regarded as personal data and may be stored and processed on a cloud platform outside of Israel without limitation.

With specific reference to privacy, in recent years, questions have arisen as to the right of employers to check the documents and emails of employees that are on the employer's devices and the extent of this right – which is a type of proprietary right of the employer (and which right stands in a certain contradiction with the employee's right of privacy).

The National Labour court, in a major decision from early 2011, has found that the balance between these two rights means that violation of the right of privacy will only be allowed in exceptional circumstances when there is a real suspicion of illegal or criminal activity on the part of the employee. In addition, the violation of the right of privacy, in order to be legitimate, has to meet certain other requirements – legitimization, proportionality, transparency, and so on.

The court has also commented that it is necessary to distinguish between the different e-mail boxes. Regarding the professional or employer mailbox, the employer is entitled to set up a supervisory and back-up system of the details of the correspondence. As for the personal or mixed workplace mailbox, the employer cannot make use as it wishes of technological means in its hands to do follow-up and the like. The employer's access to that mailbox is only permitted in exceptional circumstances where there is a real, founded and reasonable suspicion of criminal or other wrongdoings on the part of the employee. Finally there is the personal external mailbox of the employee – this is the clear personal (albeit intangible and virtual) property of the employee and the employer cannot access it.

As also noted above in Section 10.9(a), the National Labour Court has also addressed the legitimacy of using fingerprint and biometric attendance mechanisms. This later National Labour Court decision reinforces the approach taken in the case mentioned above addressing access to employee emails, with the emphasis placed on the employee's right to privacy which can only be intruded upon in limited and strictly interpreted circumstances.

22.2. Checklist of Dos and Do Nots

(a) Employers are almost always required to register the database that contains information with respect to their employees.
(b) Put in place a policy with respect to technology use and monitoring to align expectations of privacy and enforce it.
(c) Allow the individuals whose information is on the database to exercise their rights of perusal and correction.
(d) Use all the information obtained in a lawful way.
(e) The transfer of information abroad is permitted, subject to the relevant regulations.
(f) Regarding the professional or employer mailbox, the employer is entitled to set up a supervisory and back-up system of the details of the correspondence.
(g) As for the personal or mixed workplace mailbox, the employer's access to that mailbox is only permitted in exceptional circumstances where there is a real, founded and reasonable suspicion of criminal or other wrongdoings on the part of the employee.
(h) Employer is not allowed to access the personal external mailbox of the employee.
(i) Employers should seek legal advice before installing security cameras in the workplace and before installing biometric or fingerprint attendance mechanisms.

23. WORKPLACE INVESTIGATIONS FOR COMPLAINTS OF DISCRIMINATION, HARASSMENT, FRAUD, THEFT AND WHISTLEBLOWING

23.1. Overview

As already noted in Section 17.4 above, the employer has certain obligations towards the employees under the Prevention of Sexual Harassment Law, 1998. In order to fulfil these obligations, the employer is obliged to prescribe an efficient procedure for filing a complaint in respect of sexual harassment and for the examination of that complaint and to deal efficiently with cases of sexual harassment or adverse treatment. In addition, the employer is required to do everything in its power to seek to prevent a recurrence of the acts and to rectify the harm caused to the complainant as a result of the sexual harassment or adverse treatment. As also noted in Section 17.4 above, an employer who employs more than twenty-five employees is required to prescribe and publish a code of practice detailing the principal provisions of the law concerning sexual harassment and adverse treatment in the workplace and also detailing the procedures prescribed by the employer for handling complaints with respect to the same, including the appointment of a supervisor.

The employer's failure to comply with its general obligations under the Prevention of Sexual Harassment Law, 1998 is a civil wrong under the Employment (Equal Opportunities) Law. In addition, where the employer is required to publish a code of practice and fails to do so, it is liable to a fine.

As also noted above, in Section 16, employees who complain against the employer or other employees are afforded certain protection under the Protection of Employees (Exposure of Offences of Unethical Conduct and Improper Administration Law), 1997.

23.2. Checklist of Dos and Do Nots

- Be aware that employer has obligations towards the employees under the Prevention of Sexual Harassment Law, 1998 and comply with same.
- Likewise, be aware that employer has obligations towards employees under the Protection of Employees (Exposure of Offences of Unethical Conduct and Improper Administration Law), 1997 and comply with same.

24. AFFIRMATIVE ACTION/NON-DISCRIMINATION REQUIREMENTS

24.1. Overview

The Employment (Equal Opportunities) Law, 1988 does not contain a general provision concerning affirmative action with respect to non-discrimination. However, there is certain legislation, which addresses this issue.

In 2000, the Government Companies Law, 1975 was amended to provide that the Arab population (including also Druze and Circassian origin) must be appropriately represented on the board of directors or every government owned company and statutory corporation.

The Civil Service (Appointments) Law, 1959 has also been amended to allow and encourage affirmative action to insure fair representation at the workplace with respect not only to women but also to handicapped persons and to other sections of the workforce (Arab, Druze, Ethiopian employees).

The Encouragement of the Advancement and Integration of Women in the Work Force and the Adjustment of Work Places to Women's Needs Law, 2008 provides for monetary incentives to employers in the private sector who try to integrate and promote women in their business, as well as to those employers who modify the workplace and work conditions to the needs of women and parents.

The Israeli Supreme Court has also stated that affirmative action is an acceptable means to abolish discrimination between the sexes.

Reference is also made to the Employment Equal Opportunities Law, 1988, which requires that employers will ensure that persons with disabilities will be adequately represented among their employees. (See above at section 3.1.)

24.2. Checklist of Dos and Do Nots

- See also checklist to Section 17 above.
- If specific legislation applies, employer should act in accordance with the same.

25. RESOLUTION OF LABOUR, DISCRIMINATION AND EMPLOYMENT DISPUTES: LITIGATION, ARBITRATION, MEDIATION AND CONCILIATION

25.1. Internal Dispute Resolution Process

The extent to which there may be an internal dispute resolution process in place, depends largely on whether the work force is part of the unionized sector or not.

In the organized or unionized sector, the rules concerning dispute resolution are set forth in the collective bargaining agreements. The parties, who will participate in these dispute resolution proceedings, are the management and the union representatives of all levels.

There are no general internal dispute resolution processes which apply as a matter of law to employees in the non-organized sector of the workforce. These employees have to seek discussions with their employer and, failing a mutually agreed outcome, they will have no alternative but to file a case with the Labour Court assuming they have legal grounds for such a claim. However, in many high-tech companies there is a company established grievance procedure which affords workers limited rights to present their grievances to management on various levels.

In this respect, it should be remembered that when terminating an employment relationship, the employer is required to provide the employee with the opportunity of having his or her case heard by the employer (see sections 5 and 6 above), although this procedure does not amount of an internal dispute resolution procedure.

The laws prohibiting sexual harassment have required employers to establish an internal procedure for allowing workers to complain against sexual harassment. In addition, the work safety laws require the employer to establish joint management-worker safety committees, in which workers can present grievances and suggestions concerning work safety.

25.2. Mediation and Conciliation

There is no law in Israel, which requires the arbitration or mediation of labour disputes. Nevertheless, alternative dispute resolution in that field is expanding.

The parties to a dispute are not compelled to mediate prior to filing a claim with the labour courts, save in cases of collective disputes. In that case, the parties should give fifteen-day prior notice of a strike or lockout to a labour ministry mediator, so that the dispute can be mediated. Some collective disputes and other complicated disputes have also been referred to special mediation by experts in labour relations.

The Labour Courts themselves have been active in the area of ADR and very often request – on a voluntary basis – that the parties try to mediate before pre-trial hearings and hearings on the evidence. The Labour Courts have internal programmes for mediation at no cost to the parties, with lay members as mediators and also refer cases to private external mediators and mediation services. The question whether to refer a case to an internal or external mediation may depend, *inter alia*, on the amount of the claim.

The courts have also established departments to handle case management, including referring cases to private mediation and arbitration. The Labour Courts have adopted an ADR of the 'many door courthouse', including mediation, arbitration, early neutral evaluation, pre-trial hearings and trials before the court panel (judges and lay members).

As far as conciliation is concerned, this is regulated under the Settlement of Labour Disputes Law, 1957. Under this Law, a 'labour dispute' is defined as a dispute between an employer and his employees or part of them or between an employer and an employee's organization or between an employers' organization and an employees' organization but does not include an individual dispute as to any of the following:

(a) the conclusion, renewal, alteration or cancellation of a collective agreement;
(b) the determination of terms of employment;
(c) the engagement or non-engagement of employees and the termination of employment;
(d) the determination of rights and obligations arising from employer-employee relations.

Under that Law, the Minister of Labour and Social Affairs is required to appoint a Chief Labour Relations Officer (Chief Officer) and labour relations officers. This Law also provides that any party to a labour dispute may give notice of the dispute to the Chief Officer. It further provides that a party to a dispute is bound to give the other party and the Chief Officer notice of every strike or lockout, as the case may be, at least fifteen days before the beginning of such strike or lockout (unless a collective agreement contains a different provision in which case such provision shall apply). The Chief Officer can decide whether to conciliate in the dispute – and if so, the Chief Officer will take on the function of conciliator (unless this function has been assigned to another person).

The conciliator is required to do his or her best to settle the dispute by negotiation and may hold meetings with the parties (together or separately, hear their arguments and proposals for settlement and submit his or her own proposals), require the parties to give a reasoned answer to the arguments of the other party, take opinion of experts and representatives of employees' and employers' organizations, examine the economic position of the undertaking in which the dispute exists, and so on. In order to carry out these functions, the conciliator may obtain any testimony – written or oral – and examine any person, summon any person to attend the conciliation meeting to give evidence or to produce a document and examine them, require any witness to confirm their evidence by oath or affirmation, make an order compelling a person to attend before him if such person has not so attended in answer to a summons, impose a fine on a person who has not justified their non-compliance to give evidence on oath or produce documents.

If the parties reach an agreement for settlement of the labour dispute, whether of their own accord or upon proposal of the conciliator, the parties or the conciliator shall draw up a written agreement setting out the conditions for the settlement – this agreement is to be signed by the parties and attested by the signature of the conciliator.

If a settlement agreement is not signed between the parties within fourteen days from the date on which the parties were first summoned to appear before the conciliator, the latter shall terminate the conciliation and a report is filed with the Chief Officer. The Chief Officer may propose to the parties the resumption of the conciliation and if they consent, it will be resumed.

If the parties do not sign a settlement agreement, anything said by the parties and any evidence given or proposal made in the course of the conciliation shall not bind the parties and shall not be used as evidence in any arbitration under the Settlement of Labour Disputes Law, 1957 (see on arbitration, Section 25.3 below).

25.3. Arbitration

In addition to the possibility to refer cases to mediation as mentioned in Section 25.2 above, cases are referred to arbitration.

While ADR is generally voluntary and not binding, there is an exception where the parties have agreed in advance that the arbitrator's decision will be binding on them.

Note that, under the Settlement of Labour Disputes Law, 1957, certain matters can be referred to arbitration under that Law. These matters are: any labour dispute (as defined in the Law, see Section 25.2 above) which the parties have consented in writing to refer to arbitration under that Law or any labour dispute which according to a collective agreement is to be referred to arbitration and in which the arbitrator[s] or the manner of their appointment has not been determined or in which the manner of appointment has been determined but they have not been appointed within a reasonable time or have not terminated the arbitration within a reasonable time.

Either party to such a dispute under the Settlement of Labour Disputes Law, 1957 which is a matter for arbitration may deliver a notice of the dispute to an officer (i.e., a labour relations officer appointed under that Law). The Chief Officer shall appoint an arbitral panel for the dispute (comprising of three members) or may assume the function of sole arbitrator or appoint a labour relations officer to act as sole arbitrator. A person who has acted as conciliator in a labour dispute may not act as arbitrator in the same dispute without the written consent of the parties.

The arbitral panel or sole arbitrator may deliberate and decide in accordance with any enactment, collective agreement or trade practice (meaning a practice or custom existing with regard to the subject matter of the arbitration) and if these provide no solution to the issue, may decide according to justice and fairness.

The powers of the arbitral panel and sole arbitrator are much the same as those of the conciliator (see Section 25.2 above). The arbitral panel is not bound by rules of evidence but is to act in the manner deemed by it most conducive to the clarification of the matter and the panel shall itself prescribe rules of procedure if they have not been prescribed in the Law itself or by regulations promulgated pursuant to the Law. Facts which come to the knowledge of a member of an arbitral panel in the course of the arbitration and which are not generally known shall be treated as secret – a violation of this provision can result in imprisonment of one year or a fine.

An arbitration award under the Law is valid for one year from the day in which it is given unless a shorter period is specified in the award and it has the effect of a contract or of a collective agreement between the parties to the arbitration.

25.4. Litigation

The enactment of the Labour Courts Law, 1969 provided for a separate judicial system dedicated to individual and collective labour disputes and issues. The Israeli Labour Courts have played a significant role in the development of labour and social security law in Israel.

The Labour Court System comprises of first instance trial level (namely, five Regional Labour Courts) and an appeals level (the National Labour Court). The National Labour Court sits in Jerusalem.

The Regional Labour Court bench is composed of one professional judge and two lay members (one from employee representatives and one from employers representatives). The National Labour Court bench is composed of three professional judges and two lay members. In criminal cases there are no lay members – only the judges hear these cases and there is an appeal as of right to the National Labour Court. In national wide collective disputes, the National Labour Court bench is composed of three professional judges and four lay members.

The jurisdiction of the Labour Courts is broad. It includes jurisdiction over individual disputes between workers and employers; interpretation and application of protective labour laws; jurisdiction over collective disputes and over disputes between a union and its members or an employer and its association; jurisdiction over issues concerning pensions, discrimination in the workplace, administrative matters relating to employees (such as where job tenders may be required and the application of the same), occupational safety and health, employment agencies, protection for migrant workers, social security and the State medical insurance.

With regard to claims based on tort, the Labour Courts have jurisdiction over such actions where they are related to a labour dispute. Thus claims based on trespass, breach of statutory duty, inducing breach of contract may be brought before the Labour Courts where they are related to a labour dispute. The Labour Courts also hear cases concerning the ratification or cancellation of an arbitration decision.

In addition to acting as an appellate court, the National Labour Court also has original jurisdiction over nationwide strikes and collective disputes.

As a general rule, it is not possible to appeal a decision of the National Labour Court. However, a party may petition the Supreme Court of Israel, sitting as a High Court of Justice, to hear a petition relating to constitutional issues or important questions of labour law. The Supreme Court of Israel has handed down important judgments on labour or social security law matters.

There are specific regulations (promulgated pursuant to the Labour Courts Law) applying to the procedures before the Labour Courts. The intention is that these regulations will be more simple to understand than the procedural regulations applicable to the regular courts in Israel. It should be noted that, by section 33 of the Labour Courts Law, the Labour Courts are empowered – in any procedural matter not regulated by the Labour Courts Law or its regulations – to decide according to what seems just and fair. Note also that, pursuant to section 32 of the Labour Courts Law, the courts are not bound by the laws of evidence (although in practice the Labour Courts will apply the basic rules of evidence, while sometimes being more liberal in the admission of evidence).

25.5. Fines, Penalties and Damages

Not applicable.

25.6. Checklist of Dos and Do Nots

- Establish an internal procedure for allowing workers to complain against sexual harassment that is compliant with legal requirements.
- If applicable, establish joint management-worker safety committees, in compliance with the work safety laws in which workers can present grievances and suggestions concerning work safety.

26. EMPLOYER RECORDKEEPING, DATA PROTECTION AND EMPLOYEE ACCESS TO PERSONNEL FILES AND RECORDS

26.1. Overview

In addition to the employer recordkeeping requirements (see, for example, those mentioned in sections 3, 4 and 10 above), the employer should ensure that each employee reviews, updates if necessary and signs off on a Form 101 (employee card). The Form 101 is an employee statement regarding his or her personal details during the current tax year must be completed at beginning of each calendar year.

26.2. Personnel Files

Please refer to Section 22 above.

26.3. Confidentiality Rules

Please refer to Section 22 above.

26.4. Employee Access

Please refer to Section 22 above.

27. REQUIRED NOTICES AND POSTINGS

27.1. Overview

The main notices and postings, which an employer is required, as a matter of law or regulation, to provide its employees are set forth below. This does not constitute a complete list of all the notices and postings, which an employer may be required to provide in any given employment relationship, but rather is a summary of the minimum, major notices and postings:

– Notification to candidate employees of the progress of the employment application. See section 3.8 above.
Notice of terms and conditions of employment – see Section 2.2 above.
– Notice of termination – there are minimum prior notice period requirements by law and the employment contract may provide for a longer period – see sections 5 and 6 above.
– Notice upon termination – the employer should provide the employee with a notice of the period of employment (date of commencement of employment and date of termination). In addition, upon termination of the employment agreement, the employer might be required to provide a letter for the pension fund or managers insurance company – see sections 5 and 6 above.
– Enhancement of Enforcement of Labour Law 2011 – a notice should be put up in the place of the party ordering the manpower services and accessible to all manpower contractor employees informing them of their rights and how they may investigate the same.
– Salary or wage slips – these should contain the details as required by law – see sections 10.9 and 26 above.
– Notice in workplace of the minimum wage. See section 10.2 above.
– Harassment – a notice should be put up in the place of the employer and accessible to all employees containing information of the sexual harassment officer within the employer's business and the complaints procedure – see sections 17.4 and 23 above.
– Smoking notices should put up in the place of the employer – see Section 18 above.

27.2. Checklist of Dos and Do Nots

– It is good practice to review, and update if required, on a regular basis the notices and posting requirements.

www.ingramcontent.com/pod-product-compliance
Lightning Source LLC
Chambersburg PA
CBHW071354230926
51846CB00002B/547
9789403504308